The
Lazy Girl's
Guide to Success

Anita Naik

PIATKUS

Visit the Piatkus website!

Piatkus publishes a wide range of bestselling fiction and non-fiction, including books on health, mind, body & spirit, sex, self-help, cookery, biography and the paranormal.

If you want to:
- read descriptions of our popular titles
- buy our books over the internet
- take advantage of our special offers
- enter our monthly competition
- learn more about your favourite Piatkus authors

VISIT OUR WEBSITE AT: www.piatkus.co.uk

For Joe

contents

acknowledgements

For Jane, Emma, Jenni, Julie and Charlotte, all of whom drip success in a variety of fields from career to finances, to motherhood, to fitness and beyond.

introduction

'What I'd give to be successful,' a friend recently said to me as she bunked off work for the day and lolled about in the park, laughingly recalling how she'd given a presentation with a hangover, and had her bank cards swallowed by an ATM machine because she was so overdrawn. 'And you know what, I really feel like I am on the edge of getting there,' she confided with a glint in her eye. I didn't like to point out the obvious that she was certainly teetering on the edge of something but it probably wasn't success, because, after all, who am I to pop her fantasy success balloon.

However, if you've picked up this book then it's likely you're yearning to grab success in one or all areas of your life, or feeling somewhat stuck in your pursuit of it. If so, it's worth knowing that I'm probably going to pop a few of your balloons in the process of getting you from where you are now to where you want to be. If you want to be successful then you need to be prepared for some lazy girl truths of the hard kind, such as whereas it is possible to take certain short cuts to success, sitting on the couch, eating doughnuts and watching TV all day is not the way to do it. Neither is moaning that other people have it easier than you (OK some people probably do, but what's that got to do with your life?), or constantly telling yourself you'll start your success venture tomorrow or the day after, and/or blaming other people for your failures.

If the latter is your whinge of choice, it might help to know that an international study on what makes rags-to-riches multimillionaires successful is a general willingness to take responsibility for their failures and learn from them, and it is this one attribute that has set them aside from people who haven't reached their goals. This is good news for anyone, because even the laziest of the lazy can do this – and, probably, while sitting on the couch eating doughnuts!

But before we get into the logistics of finding and being successful, let's start with a simple question: 'What is success?' For some people it's being able to retire at 35, for others a match made in heaven, and for others a bank account filled with ample amounts of cash and/or a career with piles of accolades. Your definition of success may vary from all of those, and even from your friends and family, but whatever it is, it should be about more than status and money. Real and lasting success in life is about a multitude of things, and although I say go for it if your dream is to be an Oscar-winning actress or the new star of *Pop Idol*, bear in mind that pursuing just one thing, such as fame or money, or even love, won't make you feel successful even if you make it to the top of the ladder. This is because true success encapsulates all areas of your life.

'But success is all down to luck,' say many people, including one friend who justifies her lack of success to the fact that she's unlucky in love, unlucky in her job choices and unlucky that she was destined to have a size 10 top and a size 14 bottom no matter how much exercise she puts herself through. If, like my friend, you think you've been dealt a hard hand in life (and, let's be honest, some people do have harder lives than others), success may indeed be harder for you to reach. However, to paraphrase a popular saying, the funny thing about lucky people is that the harder they work the luckier they get! Meaning, if you want to be a successful lazy girl you have to be willing to work harder than you do right now; that is, you have to get up and put some effort in to reaching your goals.

Unlike other motivational books, however, I won't be advocating a personality transplant or daring to suggest that you give up everything you like doing so that you can reach the stars (or whatever your definition of success is). Instead, this book is about manageable success (meaning you can take it to the max or turn it down low and just tinker with your life). Although, bear in mind that the amount of results you achieve equals the amount of effort you put in, so the less you put in the less you'll get out of it.

You can also take this book in a number of ways. You can read it from cover to cover and treat it as your new best friend, or use it on a dip in-dip out basis – focusing on the area you are most concerned with. If you're still asking yourself, 'Why should I bother?' ponder this: money and fame aside, feeling that you're successful makes you feel good about yourself. It boosts your self-esteem, keeps away the blues and generally helps you find a sense of worth that no one can take away, no matter how lazy you choose to be in life – and what could be better than that?

chapter one

What is success?

When you imagined your future you probably imagined fame, glory, Mr Right on your arm, loads of money and a life of glamour – in other words you imagined success, success, and success. And who can blame you, because when it comes down to it most of us want to make it (whatever 'make it' means to you). The problem is that if you're a lazy kind of girl it's likely that most of your best success stories lie in your head, because you're either (a) too busy to stop what you're doing and think about what you'd like to be doing; or (b) too lazy to put some effort into going after what you want. Which is why the world is full of people who say, 'I could have been a pop singer/ movie star/millionaire if only I'd got my chance/had a lucky break/had some money behind me'! However, dig a bit deeper and their 'if onlys', tend to really be, 'if only I'd got off the sofa a bit more often and tried a bit harder'.

And that, in a nutshell, is where success lies. Dreams are great, and, let's face it, you've got to have one if you want to be successful, but success doesn't just come knocking on your door along with your evening takeaway. (Having said that I do know someone whose Mr Right was the pizza delivery man.) It takes graft, hard work, effort and, of course, much planning. If that sounds at odds with your lazy girl status think again, because you don't have to be a superwoman juggling four kids, a multimillion-dollar business and a glamorous social world to be successful in life.

Success is something very personal. For some people it is about money and designer clothes, but for others it's about personal happiness and/or physical glory. It's up to you to choose what success means to you and then it's important to define it in terms of your own life and your own goals. If you let other people – such as your friends, family or the world in general – determine what it means for you, you're likely to end up with a goal you don't really want, zero motivation, and ultimately frustration and unhappiness when you cross the finish line.

So ask yourself:

What does success mean to you?

The easiest way to determine this is to think back over your life to those fleeting moments when you felt your heart leap with excitement, and satisfaction surging through your body. Did it happen when you won a prize at school or did something you were scared of? Or perhaps it was when someone you fancied asked you out, or when you fulfilled an ambition? That surge of pleasure is where your success goals lie, so you need to ask yourself whether you're really after achievement, glory, a financial reward or a social one.

Why do you want to be successful?

If the answer is that you don't, or that it doesn't really matter to you, but you're reading this book, then you're not being 100 per cent honest with yourself. In fact you're being 'passive ambitious'. This is where you pretend you're not really after success because you're actually too afraid to get stuck in and try, and as a result you have a nice safety net when you fail. Clues that this describes you are a feeling of envy and bitterness when people get what you secretly want and a feeling of being left behind by your peer group. The answer is simple: get real. You're reading a book on success because that's what you're after – commit 100 per cent or forget about it.

Other reasons you may want success include proving something to your family, or ex-partners, to get a life

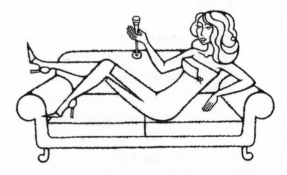

you've never had, and/or to achieve some level of personal satisfaction. These aspects all drive people towards success, and are good motivators. However, it's important also to make sure that your goals make you happy as well as other people, or else your satisfaction at your eventual success will be short-lived.

How will you know when you've made it?

It sounds like a bizarre question, but to feel successful you have to have markers along the way or a set point to know when you've made it. Having said that, while set points do work – such as, 'I will be successful when I get a job that earns me 100k a year' – you'll probably find that success is also addictive. Meaning, it's a bit like climbing a mountain: you get to the top, feel the joy of success and then think, 'What next?' The 'what-next?' for you might be maintenance; for example, staying where you are in terms of weight, or making sure your relationship stays great, or it could be striving for a completely new goal. (Like many entrepreneurs such as Richard Branson, who is currently planning on taking tourists into space.) Or it might be setting a new goal within the same frame, such as having written one successful book you want to ensure you keep writing more.

tip

Lazy or not, if you want to be successful you have to apply ample effort in whatever direction your goals lie.

Stop whining – start doing!

Rate your success quota right now and it's likely that it's less than perfect, never mind less than successful. In truth, studies show that over 86 per cent of us dream of having a different and more successful life than we have now. Meaning, we're dissatisfied, fed up and generally peeved at what our lives have turned out to be. All this can change in an instant if you decide that success is something you want to go after, and, contrary to popular belief, it's never too late, you're never too old, and you'll never be too busy to go for it. In fact, life is full of examples of people who have become successful in spite of (or maybe because of) all of the above, and whereas it's annoying to hear of the woman who held down three jobs, did voluntary work and still found time to write a best-selling novel *and* marry Mr Right, these examples show it can be done.

From a lazy girl point of view you thankfully don't have to transform yourself from couch potato to Wonder Woman to be successful, but you do have to change your mindset and add a bit of oomph to your life. This means stop punishing yourself for not being successful if you haven't ever tried. Instead, do something proactive that moves you from where you are now to where you want to be – and stop whining about your life. This can be something as simple as applying yourself at work and actually volunteering for work assignments, to actively asking people out when you're single. Every little bit of action you take brings you closer to success, in the same way that every piece of inaction keeps you further away from what you want.

So start by asking yourself:

- What is it about my current life that is getting me down?

- What area do I secretly yearn to be successful in?

- What areas of my life could do with a little success-boost?

- What would make me feel successful?

tip

Every bit of positive action you take brings you closer to success, in the same way that every piece of non-action keeps you further away from what you want.

This last question in particular is important because there are varying degrees of success, so it's vital to determine what would make you feel successful and not let it be dictated to you by outside sources. Remember: your schooldays are over, so there are no criteria to measure your success by, except the ones that you set for yourself. Meaning, you're the one who can now determine what equals success and what equals failure, so work out what your finishing line is and aim towards that.

Of course, this isn't always easy, because there's always some irritating person who's eager to point out that your goals are mediocre or you should try harder. The aim with being successful, however, is not to gallop over someone else's finish line but to make it past your own, which is how even the laziest girl can end up being the Queen of Success.

Know your limitations and then get over them

Research shows that we're all made differently and all work in different ways. It's hardly rocket science, and yet society still tries to make us all fit into one box of success; that is, you're successful if you earn large amounts of money; you're successful if you have a good career; you're successful if you can fit into a size 10 pair of jeans; and you're a success if you are married and have kids, and so on. This is, of course, rubbish, but can be easy to believe when you don't feel you fulfil any notion of what it means to be a success.

This is just one reason why it pays to get to grips with your strengths, weaknesses and different skills, because once you know what it is that makes you tick (or what doesn't) you can start making your instincts work for you. And once you take a long, hard look at yourself you may well find that what you feel are your strengths are in fact your weaknesses, and vice versa. For example, you may feel your weakness is that you procrastinate, but the hidden strength here could well be that procrastinating gives you the vital time you need to evaluate a situation properly. So ask yourself:

- Are you someone who throws herself in at the deep end with new ventures? If so, people are probably always telling you to slow down and look before you leap. However, you're what is known as a quick starter and this is how you achieve your best results: by following your instincts.

- Are you someone who needs to research things heavily and read lots of books before you begin? If so, people assume you're a procrastinator when in fact you're simply fact-driven and need to know the basics before attempting something new. Be true to yourself, as this is your best way of achieving success.

- Are you someone who literally has to 'see' what's happening before getting involved? If so, you're what is known as visually led: you have to watch what's happening before you can implement your goals. Again, this is an instinctive action, and one that may not have left you academically successful but can work well in life.

- Are you someone who likes to seek expert advice and tuition before starting something and only then can proceed? If so, your best chance of success is to use this technique in your goals and then follow it through.

Once you've worked out what you suck at and what you excel at, the next stage is to give yourself a dream overhaul.

This is because whereas there are certain dreams that could equal success and are worth pursuing, there are also certain dreams that should just stay dreams, and knowing the difference between the two is the key to success.

We've all watched those programmes where hopelessly untalented people audition for a chance to be a pop star, actress and/or dancer with the belief that they really, truly could make it. Amusing viewing aside, what's heart rending about their pursuit of success is that nowhere along the line did they realistically look at whether they had any talent in this area.

Be realistic

The fact is you have to be realistic when you're going after success, because you can't be a catwalk model if you're under 1.62m (5ft 4in), you can't be a singer if you are tone deaf and you can't be a doctor if you can't pass exams. It seems obvious, but many people pursue dreams because the dreams are based on what they want, rather than what they can do. Again, knowing the difference and being able to work out honestly if your goals are viable or not is the key to being successful.

That doesn't mean that you have zero chance of being successful just because you've realised you'll never be a

tip

To feel successful in your life you have to follow your wants and needs – focus on what it is that makes you happy and the people who make you the happiest and you're destined to feel successful!

movie star, but more that you have to reassess your vision of success. Don't be an all-or-nothing kind of girl – if you can't act, could you work in the movie business in some other way? What skills, talents and strengths do you have that could help you find success in another field? What would make you feel successful if you didn't fulfil your number-one dream? Above all, remember that just because one door closes, it doesn't give you an excuse to head back to the couch. Get up and open another one and keep opening doors until you find what it is you want.

Beat your inner demons

❮ *I never saw myself as someone who could do anything. I failed most of my exams at school and have always worked in shops. Then a friend suggested I make the most of my people skills and be a social worker, and I spent two years giving her every reason why I'd fail, then one day I got bored with moaning and signed up for a course. Five years later I'm qualified and working in the field, and I love it!* ❯

Liz, 32

This is another variation on being positive, but more important because it's about expecting a good outcome. If you think you attract losers in love, let money slip through your fingers and can't do more than be someone's assistant, that's the outcome you'll get. To be successful you need to silence the voice within that tells that you you're rubbish, and basically have a vision of yourself having a successful outcome. This is how athletes win gold medals, boxers beat their opponents and writers like J.K. Rowling go on to write a best-seller despite rejections.

Seeing yourself as someone who not only has the potential to be successful but can also be successful is vital, and the way to do this is to remind yourself of what you're capable of and what you've been successful in so far. One fatal mistake people make is to assume that just because they find something easy it's not a talent or a success. For example, you may be an excellent friend and are always there for others in their time of need, but if you're lacking in confidence and feel you haven't achieved other goals it's likely you don't see this as a success or something to be proud of. So start valuing yourself and acknowledging your successes.

- Think of three things that you were successful in – these can be passing exams, a driving test, standing up for yourself, asking someone out, losing weight or getting a job, and remind yourself of them when you feel like a failure.

- Think of three times when you attempted something new and had a gut feeling it was going to work out, and it did.

- Think of three times you succeeded in something you were scared of because you told yourself you could do it, and use that to push yourself.

- Think of three successful people you admire, and every time you feel yourself backing out of something think about how they would react and respond, and use that to motivate yourself.

Silence the critic within

1. Answer every negative thought with a positive one. This trains your brain to question what you're telling it, so that you don't immediately give up but think: what's making me back down? Is it fear, anxiety and/or panic, and what can I do to counter it?

2. Source your voice. Meaning, work out whose critical voice you're hearing. Often the critic in our head is the voice of a judgemental parent/boyfriend/teacher/friend and isn't ours at all, which means you can choose to silence it.

3. Question your self-beliefs. Are you really slack at your job, lazy about relationships and greedy about food, or is that something you've been told about yourself and never bothered to question?

Get motivated for success

Whereas you're the only person who can really say what success means to you, there's one definite thing you have to accept about being successful, and that is that you have to work at it. Sure, there are people who look as if they have done it all effortlessly, but behind their public façade they've gone through as much blood, sweat and tears as the next person, whether their aim was to end up with a decent relationship or a successful business. This is because success doesn't come easy to anyone, and, in a way, you don't want it to, because half the enjoyment of feeling successful is knowing that you deserve it because you've worked hard, motivated yourself and beat others on your way to the top.

This is why in deciding what it is you want to be successful in you have also to get to grips with motivation and find out what incentive you're going to use to drive yourself forward. For some people, negative associations work, such as losing face, becoming bankrupt or being left alone, whereas for others positive rewards such as money, prizes and being held in esteem by others do the trick.

Motivator 1: put your thoughts into action

The process of making your goals happen occurs when you start to make them real, so arm yourself with a notebook and write down what you want to achieve, and be as specific as possible (for more on this see the relevant chapters). The aim here is to see your final reward in big bold letters, as it's this that will motivate you. Is it the thought of being famous, being in love or fitting into skinny jeans? What would make you feel rewarded and justify the hard work you've put in?

Motivator 2: get inspired

Inspiration is a major motivator – look at all the people who lose weight when their favourite celebrity does, or all the people who start their own businesses after reading about someone else's success. If you feel stuck and/or demotivated, you need to get inspired in whatever way you can. Go to the gym, listen to music, read magazines and books or even take some time out from your life. The idea is to do something that causes you to think, respond and act.

Motivator 3: choose a short-term and a long-term goal

These two things are essential when working towards success, because if you don't reap some rewards for your hard work in the short term, you'll give up in the long term. For example, if your goal is to write a novel, your short-term goal should be either to join a creative writing course or to start writing; your long-term goal should be to have your writing published. Each week your short-term goal should change (because you've hopefully reached it) and bring you closer to your long-term goal.

Motivator 4: do something every day

Wait until you're ready to do something and it's likely you'll never to do it, which is why there's nothing like doing something to get you motivated. For example, if you loathe exercise and hate the thought of getting to the gym but know you have to in order to lose weight, you know that it's pointless to wait until you feel like it because you never will. However, if you make yourself go, the very act of doing it will encourage you to keep going. The same principle works for career success, love success and financial success – do something every day towards your vision of success and you'll not only stay motivated but also up your chances of a successful outcome.

Be prepared

Whatever the source of your motivation, in order to use it effectively you also have to:

Be committed to your idea

Being half-hearted about what you want is a recipe for disaster. No one ever got successful being half-committed to what they wanted. Again, it can help to have a few successful role models here so that you can check out their stories to see what they had to do to reach their goals. You'll see that in every case they were 100 per cent committed to getting what they wanted. This tactic works whether you're aspiring to be the next Oprah Winfrey or trying to find love.

Have faith in yourself

This is another essential component of staying motivated and reaching your goals. Having faith in yourself is about knowing that despite the past and what others say, you can make it. It's about believing in yourself, especially when things go wrong and success seems further away than ever.

Expect annoying times

(Also known as: no matter how hard you work and how committed you are there will be annoying times when you doubt your objectives, worry that you're going about things the wrong way and wish you'd never started.) This is where your bounce-back gene needs to kick in. You have to be able to pick yourself up and start again. This is important, because life is tough like that sometimes, but it's what results you get when you go after anything that is really important. So don't give up, because for every step back you'll always end up taking two steps forward.

Love your objective

Sometimes people find that their successes leave them cold. This is because they didn't really go after what they loved. Wanting to be in a pop band because you want to be famous, or wanting to work as a banker so that you could be rich, or wanting to be skinny so that people will find you attractive aren't incentives enough to make success rewarding. Choose your goal carefully so that when you get there (and you will if you follow the tips in this book) all the hard work and graft is actually worth it and you're glad you've gone for it.

Motivated people are:

- Encouraging
- Fun
- Open to new things
- Optimistic
- Realistic
- Productive
- Happy
- Interesting
- Dynamic
- Active

Success troubleshooting

OK, so you may think it's way too early in the book to have a section about troubleshooting when you're not yet successful, but as the popular saying goes: to be prepared is to be forewarned. Being successful can be many things – exciting, thrilling, and mind-blowing – but, and this is a large BUT, it comes with a new set of problems that may have you wondering why you even bothered to change your life in the first place, so here's all you need to know about problems with success, as you work your way upwards:

Success is hard to live up to

tip

Competitive people are competitive because they're aiming to get to the top as fast as possible – remember you don't have to compete with them!

Somewhere between becoming a success and leaving the old you behind, you'll find that what people say about you and how you feel about yourself changes. This is because people get envious and threatened by your success and/or you'll start thinking that it's been a fluke and that somehow you're faking it and will one day be exposed as the loser. The good news is that this is a very common feeling and much felt by lazy girls in particular. As you begin to trust in your new-found success and see it lasting you'll be more willing to own it – and believe you deserve it – and then you'll find your new label more comfortable, and so will others. In the meantime don't be pathetically grateful or tell people you were just 'lucky'; if you've made it big in some area of your life, be thankful, be gracious and revel in it – after all you deserve it.

Other people's envy

Of course another nasty by-product of success is jealousy. There's nothing like hitting it big in the financial stakes, career stakes or even body-and-love stakes to have your best friends and family turning green with envy. Some will try to hide it (usually badly), some will make sniping backhanded remarks and some will act as if you've single-handedly stolen what was rightfully theirs! You can deal with envy in a number of ways: you can either pretend it's not happening, or feel bad that people are envious, and let them treat you badly – or you can simply confront it. The latter is the best way (and also the hardest way) simply because even though people will deny it at first and make you feel as if you're imagining it, eventually they'll admit defeat and confess, and then you can work through it together and move on. If you ignore it or soak it up, all that will happen is you'll either start sabotaging your success to make others happy or simply cut off ties with the jealous person, or you will lose a friend.

‘ *When I first lost weight everyone told me I looked great, but within a week certain friends suggested I'd gone too far, or looked too scrawny. One ex-friend even suggested I had an eating disorder and went*

round telling everyone. It took me a while to realise I was doing fine and that it was envy and jealousy speaking. ❱

Claire, 27

Dealing with competitiveness

If you've been a lazy girl all your life and have come to success late, the one area that may floor you is the competitive arena you now find yourself in. There's nothing like being successful to open your eyes up to the fact that there will always be someone nipping at your heels eager to get where you are now, and usually at your expense. Mostly you'll be fine if you keep your wits about you, and don't focus too much on what others are doing (unless it's a direct business competitor, in which case you should be 100 per cent on the case).

However, it's worth bearing in mind a couple of points about competitive people: (a) they are competitive because they're aiming to get to the top as fast as possible; and (b) their behaviour is not personal, even if it feels that way. Meaning that whereas they have their own agendas and may well be out to sabotage you, they are just fighting their own fight to get to the top. The best tactic is to either ignore them and focus solely on what you're doing, which tends to take the wind out of their sails, or confront them so that *they* know that *you* know what they're up to.

Examples that may come up are:

- People who tell you that you've lost too much weight, and that you shouldn't lose any more – and then offer you a doughnut!

- People who make you doubt your work decisions and promotions by hinting that you weren't the first choice.

- People who suggest that you don't really know your boyfriend.

- People who put down financial success, suggesting they are after something deeper!

Their motives are all the same: to destabilise you, get past you and make themselves feel better at your expense. To counteract this, use your gut instinct and work on decisions that feel right for you.

Success addiction

Experiencing success is addictive, and once you start to taste a bit of it, the desire for more and more and more will probably spread to other areas of your life. In most cases this isn't a problem, as confidence in one area does tend to spread across your life. However, don't become addicted to just going for the high. The whole pleasure of feeling successful is enjoying the climb as much as the peak; that is, how you got to where you are and what personal resources you used to get there. Just being success-focused (such as just wanting a wedding, or 100k in the bank, or a job title,

tip

For job success differentiate between a wish and a dream. A wish is a fantasy that you can enjoy in your head but in all likelihood have never done anything to work towards in your life.

or to hit a certain target weight) isn't as thrilling, as, say, knowing you worked for a year to lose 10kg (1 stone 8lb/ 22lb), or you got promoted because you're a popular member of the team.

What's more it pays to know when to stop; if the goal posts of success keep moving away from you no matter what you do, you need to focus on what's enough. The name of the game is to feel successful for yourself not to please a family member, a boyfriend or to get back at someone from your past who once slighted you.

Finally, the only way now is ...

What goes up, eventually comes down, but that doesn't mean that one day all your successes will be stripped away and you'll be back where you started, but it does mean that the success you're aiming for now won't always be the thing you feel successful about. As you change and grow older your definition of success will change, too, and your idea of what you want will change with it. Which is why people leave jobs when they're at the pinnacle of their success, or give away all their money. To feel successful for life you have to follow your wants and needs. Focus on what it is that makes you happy and the people who make you the happiest and you're destined to feel successful for life!

20 ways to

get motivated for

success

1 Develop a passion
It's hard to feel motivated if you don't feel passionate about something, because it's passion that drives us to do things. So step one to success is to find at least two consuming passions in your life. It can be food (making it rather than eating it), music, books, your career or even your love life. The more you train your mind to get passionate about things, the more likely you are to feel motivated in your life and keyed up to do things.

2 Sleep more effectively
Got no time to be successful? Think again! You may think you 'need' your sleep but if you want to feel motivated and get things done then you have to learn to sleep more effectively; that is, go to bed earlier, get up earlier and don't skip sleep for a drunken night out. Start by focusing on waking half an hour earlier in the morning and sleeping half an hour earlier at night and see how that gives you more time in the day.

3 Surround yourself with go-getting people

Meaning, mix with people who have a real verve for life and notice how your energy flags when you spend time with someone who moans all the time, or is negative about everything. These people are energy vampires and you need to keep away from them if you want to be successful. Motivated people give off energy and make you feel you can achieve anything you set your mind to. Find this type of person and stick like glue to them.

4 Work out what pushes you into action

Are you someone who is stirred into action by thinking of the worst-case scenario or the best-case scenario? Both tactics work in getting you to move your butt, but people tend to fall into one camp or the other so choose the one that works best for you.

5 Dream big, but don't be a big dreamer

Believe it or not these are two very different things. People who dream big have goals, stay motivated and go for what they want, whereas people who are big dreamers tend to live in a fantasy land rather than going after what they want, because the fantasy is just so nice and enjoyable that it's more pleasurable to muse it over and play it out in your head than make it real.

6 Have positive expectations

It's easier to be motivated to do something if you think you can reach your goals, so be a glass half-full kind of girl and imagine a positive outcome to everything you do. And while you're at it, remember: expecting the worst doesn't stop you from being disappointed when you fail; it still leaves you feeling bad and actually demotivates you.

7 Don't procrastinate all the time

Are you a big talker? Someone who is going to X, Y and Z but, weirdly, never manages to reach even X? If so, it's likely you're a full-time procrastinator, someone who has amazingly brilliant ideas but can't put their plans into action because they are afraid of failing. Like a big dreamer, procrastinating continuously is the enemy of success – less thinking, more doing!

8 Dangle a carrot in front of your nose

The trouble with having zero motivation is it eventually becomes a stick to hit yourself with. So if you feel guilty, bad and fed up with your lack of zest, change tactics and dangle a carrot in front of your face instead. Enticement of a reward works better as a motivator than guilt, whether your goal is to lose weight, get a new job or balance your accounts.

9 Motivate other people

There's nothing more likely to get you feeling motivated than to motivate others, so be someone's cheerleader and you'll discover the power of motivation and how it could work for you. Being a mentor, or a positive friend helps people highlight their assets, build goals and go after their dreams. Try it – you'll be surprised by how much rubs off.

10 Do something every day

It's hard to be motivated when you're in awe of the bigger picture, so every day write down three things you have to do that will take you closer to your end goal, and make sure you do them.

11 Energise yourself

It's hard to stay focused if you feel tired and exhausted all the time. This means that if you are trying to motivate yourself you need to lose a few of your lazy girl habits. Eat well, sleep effectively (see above) and drink lots of water, and you'll find you have the energy to get up and do things.

12 Don't focus on past failures

We all focus on what we've done wrong or what we should have done, and forget all the decisions in our life that went right for us, so ditch your regrets, as they are major demotivators. The next time you feel bad about the past, immediately recall all the things you have achieved and revel in feeling good.

13 Be positively realistic
This is a variation on being positive. Being positively realistic means knowing yourself and understanding your strengths and weaknesses so that your goals are reachable, not unattainable.

14 Inspire yourself
Associate a strong enough vision to your goal and you'll feel motivated to go after it. So instead of thinking, I should get to the gym because it's the right thing to do, read up on people who have changed their looks and bodies, get inspired by their stories and create a picture of the new you to work towards (this technique works whatever your goal is).

15 Bounce back
If at first you don't succeed, don't just sit on the sofa – get up and keep trying. Success doesn't just happen because you've decided you're going to go for it, you need to make an effort, and keep making an effort even when you fall flat on your face. Keep bouncing back and you'll get there in the end.

16 Finish what you start

This is a major motivation tip, because if you have trouble with motivation it's also likely you have trouble finishing what you start. If this is the case, train yourself to finish things – even if you've lost interest. Getting to the end of a task teaches you that you are someone who is capable of completing tasks.

17 Get a cheerleading squad

(Also known as: surrounding yourself with people who encourage and support you.) Many of us have good friends who are actually objectors – people who are always telling you why you can't do something or giving you excuses to give up on your dreams. In order to make it you need to find a support team. See how it affects your life for the better.

18 Play to your strengths

Like giving up booze or going on a diet, in order to stay motivated you need to be able to work out your weak spots and stay away from them. For example, if you know your motivation flags in the afternoon, set all your go-for-it tasks in the morning. If Fridays are your lazy days then make sure you haven't scheduled an important meeting that day. Play to your strengths and you'll boost your motivation.

19 Keep going

Staying motivated is hard, especially when the days get hotter and everyone else is taking it easy and having a good time. However, these are the days to watch, because while you can take a break, don't take your eye off the ball for too long, or else you'll feel back at square one.

20 Ask for help

If you're losing momentum, it can help to ask a friend or expert along to help either to boost your confidence or literally tackle a task with you. This can help make your task fun, keep your goals upbeat and enable you to see the bigger picture, just when you feel your motivation slipping away.

chapter two

Career success

Are you seriously too lazy to think about your career, or is your laziness a sign that you don't believe you are the career type or even want to be the career type? Or maybe you once had a very non-lazy attitude to work but day-to-day slogging and company politics have beaten you down? If so, it's likely you're suffering from career ambivalence – where you don't exactly hate work, but you don't love it either. Meaning, you're well and truly stuck in a rut and could do with revitalising your career.

Just like success in other areas of life, the definition of what would make your job successful for you should be dependent on you and no one else. It shouldn't be determined by job titles, how much you get paid and how others feel about your job, unless you want it to be. Success could be getting a job you enjoy, or finally getting into a career you've always dreamed of, or even discovering that you're good at something and are able to make a living from it. It could even be something as simple as having a job that makes you want to get up in the mornings.

Think it's too late for you to have career success? Well, think again. You are never too old, or too anything to have missed the career-success boat completely (let's face it, even people who retire can suddenly find career success in a whole new field). And while there are certain careers that you may no longer be eligible for – such as child star (under 12), supermodel (under 18) and possibly Olympic athlete (although British athlete Kelly Holmes did manage it at 35) – everything else is out there for the taking. You can still be a star of some sort, write a best-seller, win an acting award, start your own business, be a lawyer, teacher, or fashion buyer, make-up artist, or even sales manager of the year if that's what you want.

You could even go back to school and retrain or learn a new language, or you could head off for career success in another country or even beat your evil boss at his own game and get promoted above him. No door is closed to you if you're willing to get off the lazy couch and investigate what's really out there.

Your working life

You will spend five days a week or approximately 40 years of your life working, so you owe it to yourself to make sure that:

- You enjoy what you're doing.
- You feel valued at work.
- You're rewarded properly for your work.
- Your work gives you a sense of achievement.
- You feel you're doing something worthwhile.
- You work with people you like.
- You aren't being taken advantage of.

Exams, academia and intelligence

Before going through the ins and outs of achieving success lazy-style, it's worth saying a few words about intelligence and academic achievement. Whether you're decades past your schooling or not, the ramifications of whether you passed your exams, applied yourself at school and/or ended up with a good-girl or bad-girl tag can, and does, last a lifetime, because it's hard to escape what you've been told about your intelligence even when sense tells you that you're long past being that moody 14-year-old.

And this works both ways, you may be the girl who everyone thought would go far, who now feels she's never reached her full potential, or the girl everyone said was dumb, who still feels she can't do anything worthwhile. These past experiences and beliefs directly affect career success and your career of choice, because if you believe you're stupid/non-academic and have no skills, or are overqualified, your lack of confidence will guide your job choices.

The key is to recognise that it's your innate skills that can actually help you achieve career success. These often have nothing to do with exams because while academic achievement is beneficial it's just one form of intelligence and won't necessarily make you successful in your career of choice. What's more, far from being static, intelligence shifts over time, and often what didn't seem to be a skill at school can be vital in the workplace, which is how people who seemed hopeless when they were 14 years old can go on to become successful when they locate their strong points.

The trick is to think about areas where you naturally shine, and not to focus on your past record.

Pinpoint your skills

- Are you someone with verbal skills?
- Are you someone with people skills?
- Do you have spatial skills, or even design skills?

These are talents that aren't recognised in the normal school system but can take you far in a career. So do yourself a favour and start looking at your innate intelligence and skills with a new eye and play to your strengths. If you're not sure what your strengths are, these are the traits and qualities that feel natural and the areas that you shine in, as well as the things that you most enjoy doing, whether they are chatting to friends or surfing the Net.

What have these got to do with work? Well, you need to

think laterally: champion Net surfers could potentially be good researchers, and eager talkers could be stars in the human-resources field. The trick is to take your strengths and find a career that suits your personality. To get there, brainstorm with friends, research at the library and think which elements of your present job best reflect who you are.

If you can do all of the above you'll kick your past record, and be a career winner whatever your academic score, because you won't end up vaguely picking a career because someone mentioned you'd be good at it (because you either failed all your exams or did brilliantly well), or muddle through doing anything that comes your way because you feel incapable of more. Keep telling yourself you can be anything you want to be, then use your brain to get there!

tip

Want to go far? Then you need to ditch a few of your lazy girl work habits such as taking 'sick' days, coasting through the afternoons, and spending 25 per cent of your working day emailing friends and surfing the Net for holiday bargains!

Where are you heading and why?

As I've said previously the key to a successful work life is to make sure that what you do for a living is in sync with who you really are. If it isn't, your working life will not only be mind-numbingly dull but also career success will always be but a distant dream. The weird fact about jobs is that most lazy girls spend more time thinking about what they are going to wear for work (and even what they're going to eat for breakfast) than what they're doing with their day and why. So ask yourself this: when was the last time you thought about where you're heading? If the answer was when you last applied for a job or got a pay rise or when your boss last irritated you, it's worth considering a new approach.

Like anything you want to succeed at, it pays to assess where you are now at least once a month.

Take time out, and ask yourself:

- Does my job fulfil me?
- Do I enjoy what I do?
- Where do I want to be in a year's time?
- What do I want more of: responsibility/money/time off/days working at home?
- What's wrong (if anything) with my current work life?
- What would make me feel successful?

The aim is not to work yourself into deep despair but to problem-solve your career woes in a logical way so that you don't find yourself in the same position five years down the line. For example, if you don't feel you are fulfilling your potential in your current job, there are three things you could you do to change:

1. Take on more responsibility by seeking out new work opportunities, volunteering for projects, and changing your reaction to work by using your initiative in projects.

2. Do a course and add more skills to your portfolio, and then seek promotion or a job change within your current company.

3. Go for a total career makeover.

Your aim should be to make a career plan with short-term and long-term goals that say more than, 'I must get through this week and make it to retirement'! Short-term goals are there to make your daily life more endurable and can be anything from finishing a project to finding a way to work with a difficult colleague. Long-terms goals should encapsulate a career plan that either moves you towards the career of your choice, a job title of your choice or a working life of your choice.

Think it can't be yours? Well, anything can be yours if you're willing to work for it. This means ditching your lazy girl work habits such as taking 'sick' days, coasting through the afternoons, opting for long lunch hours, and spending 25* per cent of your working day emailing friends and surfing the Net for holiday bargains (*statistic according to AOL). While most of the above are signs you're dissatisfied with what you're doing, they're also easy pitfalls even if you like your job, because, let's face it, everyone does it and sometimes it's better than working.

However, like the dieter who has to give up cakes and crisps to get slim, to get your career in shape you have to do less of the above and more of the work stuff. The good news is that in reality it's easier than you think to get ahead, because most people can't be bothered to do it and would rather just keep their head down and complain than tackle a difficult work problem. What's more, plenty of other people just aren't interested in being successful at work, because either they have a home life that keeps them happy enough or they simply don't have the ambition gene, which means that if you want more out of your work you're already ahead of the field.

How do you know if you're ripe for change and filled with ambition?

You're ambitious if you:

- Feel envious when people get promoted above you.
- Know in your heart you can do more and achieve more.
- Know you aren't being used to your full potential by your company.
- Feel cheated if a friend gets a better job than you.
- Worry that you're getting left behind your peer group.
- Have a career dream that hasn't yet been fulfilled.

And, contrary to popular belief, ambition isn't a dirty word. Wanting success and more glory doesn't mean you're ruthless, egotistic or conceited – it means that in your heart you know there's a part of you that hasn't yet had a chance to shine. Ambition is simply about fulfilling your desires, dreams and hopes, and that's the best kind of success to strive for.

You're passively ambitious if you:

- Wait for promotion to come to you.
- Feel bitter about other people's successes but can't be bothered to try harder at work.
- Never get round to applying for jobs because you're too busy complaining.
- Haven't updated your CV since you left school.
- Assume that your perfect job will one day land in your lap.
- Haven't improved your skills since the day you started work.

Be what you want to be (within reason)

Studies show that whereas men will quite happily apply for the job of their dreams regardless of their skills, 90 per cent of women hold back because they fear they're not good enough. If this is you, you don't need a lesson in how to get promoted but a lesson in how to boost your self-worth. It sounds obvious, but if you wait for other people to give you value via a promotion or job title, you'll always walk around feeling a fake, no matter how far you get, and worry constantly that one day someone will expose you. This faker's syndrome is more common than you think and is the enemy of career success. The way around it is literally to see your skills and strengths, and to find valida-tion in the person you are right now, not who you could become or what your job title is or how much money you make from your work. Easier said than done I know, but to feel successful in any area of your life, you have to feel you're worthy of it, not grateful. Otherwise, you'll strive all your life for successes that will just end up making you feel empty and sad.

Having said that you can be who you want to be, it also pays to be realistic about your hopes and aspirations. If your dream is to be a movie star and you haven't acted since you were in high school, or have always been too shy to get up in front of people, then the chances are you're not going to make a very good actress. It's vital to remember that your current life is a fantastic indicator of where your interests lie. Meaning, if you say you want to write plays but never put pen to paper, or you say you want to run your own business but can't manage your bank account or balance your chequebook, then you're probably fooling yourself.

Differentiate, too, between a wish and a dream. A wish is a fantasy that you can enjoy in your head but in all likelihood have never done anything to work towards in your life. Whereas a dream is a vision that you feel pulled towards and have probably done many things leading to it in your life. Above all bear in mind that whereas the world is your oyster (within reason) a lot of people focus on success in a particular career simply because they like the idea of a particular job or the lifestyle that goes with it, even though they are not particularly interested in the actual job or have a natural talent in that field.

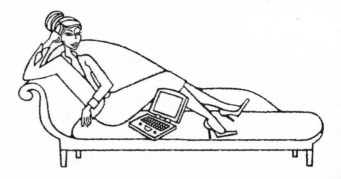

> ## *You know your dream job's right if:*
>
> - You have researched how to get into it and you know the pitfalls.
> - You're clear about what your role could be in that industry.
> - You're willing to do extra work to get into that job.
> - You feel happy when you immerse yourself in your chosen area.
> - You can see yourself in this job and see your skills working here.
> - Wanting this job is about more than money and prestige (even if they are major factors).

What do you want from a job?

This is a seemingly easy question, and somewhat essential in your quest for career success, but unfortunately it is not so easy to answer. One classic lazy girl response is to say, 'An interesting job with no stress, more money, less time at work and lots of glamour.' Sounds ideal, but let's look at all the contradictions that make such a job virtually impossible. Firstly, if you find a job interesting, then you're likely to be committed to it, which means, like it or not, there are going to be times when it is stressful (like most jobs), because stress comes not only from a workload but also from caring about what you're doing. Secondly, more money for less time working … mmm … very unlikely in this day and age, unless Hollywood actress and successful children's book writer are on your list, which is why if you're trying to change jobs and get more success you need to question how realistic your desires are before you start looking for it.

So ask yourself: what would make me feel successful in my current, or a new, career?

More money

If it's more money you're after, then you need to set yourself a top figure that you want to aim for in the long run, and a more realistic figure for your immediate job move. If you plan on staying in the same industry, look at companies that pay at the higher end of the scale and think about what new skills you'd need to get in order to land a job there. If you want a pay rise in your current job, then you need to know why you deserve it before seeing your boss. When asking for it avoid pleading poverty, making threats to leave or starting to cry. Instead make sure you have a solid reason for asking (such as you are vital to your team, you do X amount of work or you've brought in new

tip

Job satisfaction and a working life that you actually find interesting is more than vital if you don't want to be driven crazy by your job!

business) and be prepared to compromise. Finally, if you're going into a whole new field to get more money be sure there's more than cash that's enticing you to move. More money is fabulous but a high income should never be the only reason to take a job.

More kudos

A job with more status is high on many people's career-success lists, so if that's what you want you need to define what you mean by more kudos. If you're looking for promotion and more responsibility in your current position you need to think about what you need to get from A to B. Look at someone in your current dream job and ask yourself what they have that you don't. Refine and rework your skills, and put out feelers to show you're not only looking for promotion but are also doing everything you can to get it. If, however, you're looking for more kudos – as in more glamour – be sure the job you're seeking does indeed hold all you want before you go for it. Many glamorous jobs aren't so fascinating when you get down to the nitty-gritty, so do your research, and speak to people in that field before changing jobs.

More time off

If you're looking for more time off work then the first question you need to ask yourself is: can I afford it? If you can, then possible ways to escape the nine to five rat race are to work for yourself, either in a freelance capacity or by starting your own business, or working part-time. The downside of being freelance, however, is that you'll be at the mercy of others in terms of what work you get given, and may find times when you're work-free. You will also need to put in a lot of energy getting work in the first place. Part-time work is also highly variable and, although your employer might agree to you working part-time, be aware that these also tend to be the first jobs to disappear when companies restructure themselves. Finally, working for yourself is probably the best way to get more time off, BUT only in the long run, as while you're starting up you'll probably need to work harder and for longer hours.

❝ I had a fantastic job on paper – lots of money, glamorous work and lots of travelling, but when I thought about it, it wasn't what I wanted from life. I wanted something more "me" so I resigned and went travelling for a year. I came back and realised I wanted to do something more creative, so retrained as a fitness instructor. I don't get paid as much but I love it and it's totally me. ❞

Sam, 27

A more interesting career

(Meaning, you're bored with your current career of choice.) If you're after a more interesting career, you need to ask yourself what you're seeking in terms of interest. What would give you job satisfaction? Helping others, making something, creating something, or even support-ing someone? What would you find interesting? A job that encapsulates a current hobby, a job that makes you think and problem-solve, or a career that's helping others? Think about what you find interesting outside of work, in your home and in your social life, and use the answers to find a career that sums up who you are and what you want.

Above all it's vital to know what equals success in your head; otherwise you'll find that your career goal posts keep moving. Remember: one person's success at a seven-figure salary is another person's four-day week, and another per-son's job title. You have to know what equals success for you in order to feel successful. The best way to do this is to write down your top three success goals and stick to them no matter what. For example, if your aim is a for a better work-life balance, then number one on your list should be a shorter working week or a shorter workday, or even a day working from home. If money is your incentive, then salary, bonuses and additional benefits should be at the top of your list. Your decisions, choices and actions towards success and new jobs should then all be pointed in this direction. Meaning, it's no good opting for a glamorous high-powered career if you're looking to work a shorter week, and no use opting for a life in the charity sector if your aim is a private office and a seven-figure salary.

What would make your perfect job?

1. How many hours a day do you want to work?
2. How much do you want to earn?
3. Do you want to work from home or in an office?
4. Are you a team or lone player?
5. Do you want a glamorous job?
6. Do you want a job helping others?
7. Do you want a busy or slow atmosphere?
8. How important is your job title?
9. How important is the location of your job?

Utilise your strengths

If you're serious about wanting to live your dream, then stop whingeing about how rubbish your job is and/or drowning your sorrows in a bar every night, and start tapping into your work instincts and strengths, which we talked about earlier, and think about where they could lead you. For example:

- If you have a tidy desk, it's likely you have an organised mind, which makes you a methodical worker.

- If you like to sort out your work problems with colleagues, you have good interpersonal skills that make you a team player.

- If you're good at talking, you have verbal skills that can help in presentation work and selling.

- If you're good with money and computer stuff, your power lies in logic.

- If you like working on your own, you have intrapersonal intelligence, which makes you a good leader or self-employed person.

- If you're visually led – that is, you see things in pictures when you talk – your skills lie in design and practical plans.

tip

For every single interest and hobby you have (no matter how strange or bizarre) there is a related job; it's up to you to research and find it, if this is where you want your career to go.

Knowing yourself like this is the key to career success, because it stops you from drifting and letting other people make decisions for you. So if, for example, you're looking for a career change, and have highlighted your skills, the next thing to do is to think laterally about your interests.

For example:

- If you love the Internet, think about working for a Web company or becoming a Web designer.

- If you love making your house look attractive, think interior design.

- If you like being outside, a job in conservation and/or horticulture might suit.

- If you love music, then think radio producer, record shop or record company.

- If you love fashion and beauty, a career in shop management or as a beauty consultant or make-up artist might be ideal.

- If you love sports, become a PE teacher or personal trainer.

Of course, not everyone wants to make their interest a job, so if you're someone who wants to find success in their current field, the answer lies in boosting your skills (think about those areas you're weak in and sign up for a course to improve them) and your work profile. Many people don't achieve success at work, not because they're bad at what they do but simply because they get lost in the crowd. Think of how many people you know who get promoted but are rubbish at what they do. These people make it because they're either good at singing their own praises or just happen to be in the right place at the right time. If that goes against your nature, don't worry because there are other and better ways to raise your profile at work:

tip

If you want a pay rise in your current job then you need to know why you deserve it before seeing your boss; that is, you are vital to your team, you do X amount of work or you've bought in new business – and be prepared to compromise.

- Sing your praises a little (also known as: make sure key individuals know what you have done), or else your role will be instantly forgotten or claimed by someone else (more common than you think).

- Socialise at work dos: this can be a hard one, especially if you don't like small talk and hate networking. However, don't just sit in a huddle with friends, walk about, talk to your bosses and make sure people get to know you.

- Be proactive in meetings and give your opinion in a positive way. Being on time, being prepared, meeting your deadlines and being enthusiastic also count more than you would imagine.

Climbing the ladder to success

Ruthlessness and brutality aside, here's how to get to the top of the career-success ladder, lazy girl style, whether you're going for a whole new career or working your way up your current job ladder.

Know your USP

Not some weird computer term but your unique selling point. As a lazy girl it's likely that you can probably do your work in record time (to make up for the time spent skiving), or are the master of multitasking (researching and shopping on the Net anyone?). Both are excellent USPs if you sell them in the right way to your boss, and they can put you ahead of the field. Whatever you decide your unique selling point is it's important always to keep everyone's attention on it in meetings, at presentations and in your everyday work. Eventually, then, all your work colleagues and your bosses will know you for that trait and keep you in mind for tasks that highlight that skill and give you more air time. The other benefits of having a USP is it helps you to stand out from the crowd – something that is essential if you want success at work. Remember: there are probably a hundred people who can do the same thing as you, it's how you do it and how visible you are that makes all the difference. Lastly, bear in mind that this works only if your USP is related to serious work issues and not to do with things like being the queen party girl and drunkenly photocopying parts of your naked body at the office party.

Let the right people know you're ambitious

Bosses and managers aren't mind-readers, so if you're secretly ambitious they will never know, and so won't think of you when a promotion comes up. Which means that whenever you have an appraisal or meeting it pays to make your ambitions clear so that your manager can effectively manage you to success. This is what managers do, and so they need to hear what you're hoping for and why. However, be careful who you make your plans known to, the workplace can be a battlefield of backstabbing and gossip, and telling all and sundry of your plans to dominate the world will call for some major nastiness. Be vocal, but at the right time and place, and back up what you're saying with professional conduct at work and a viable plan that shows your boss that you have thought it all out.

Show people you mean business

If you've previously been known as the company slacker and you're now keen for some success, it's up to you to show people you've changed and mean business. This is easier said than done, especially as people don't like to see you change. However, it involves simple things like showing up to meetings prepared, meeting deadlines and, more importantly, taking the initiative when working and coming up with solutions.

Alongside this be someone who is pro the company, as it's company people who obviously get promoted. This doesn't mean you have to be a company woman who lives and breathes work, but simply don't be a complainer. It's easy to become the person who moans every time a new idea is put forward and is negative about everything, and think you're being proactive or playing devil's advocate; however, in your bosses' eyes you'll be labelled a trouble-maker.

> *tip*
>
> Use constructive criticism with solutions, so you'll be viewed as a 'manager' rather than a meddler.

Make an impact

… of the good variety, which means no naked tabletop dancing at the office party and no drunken kissing of the IT personnel! To make an impact, try to do things outside your frame of work that utilise your strengths and skills. If you're a very social person used to throwing parties in your private life, suggest a client evening of a different sort using your outside-work skills (within reason). If you're a bit of a social show off, volunteer for presentations and wow everyone with your humour and offbeat take on life. Even if you're quiet and shy you can suggest other ways of making an impact, perhaps a fun work newsletter or a workday out. Or even something that will benefit personnel such as a crèche, a new coffee machine, or even in-house massages/yoga lessons in the lunch hour.

Get on with your boss

We all love to moan about the people who hire us. However, be wary of doing this too loudly or too frequently, especially if you want to get a promotion. The trick is to build rapport with your boss without getting too personal. He doesn't need to know the name of your cat or that your boyfriend snores, in the same way that you shouldn't need to know personal details about him. Instead be friendly, say hello (it will go further than you think) and don't be too eager to please. Again, the name of the game is to get yourself known as someone who is friendly and easy to work with, rather than a huge suck-up!

Be interview-ready

You'd be amazed at how many people don't prepare for an interview and either try to wing it or assume that the interview will be done on their past record. Which means if you want a job badly enough you owe it to yourself to take time to prepare. This means by the time you sit down opposite your interviewer you should know: details about what the job entails; background about the company; how your skills would best fill the role in hand; and something about the brand/client/type of work you're going to be special-ising in. Then forget what's on your CV (because they should have already read it by then) and sell, sell, sell yourself. Tell your prospective employers why you have the right skills for this job and what you could bring to the company, and how, and ensure that they go away with a strong idea of how you'd fit into this role.

❛ You'd be amazed at how many people I interview who turn up and don't know what the company does, who our clients are, or have no idea what the actual job is they've applied for. Some even assume that they've got the job already. It makes me so angry because it's a complete waste of my time and theirs. ❜

Anna, corporate lawyer, 30

Look professional at all times
If you're guilty of strolling into work looking dishevelled and hung-over, it's time to change the style record,

especially if you want to climb that career ladder. That doesn't mean you have to go against type and wear what the management clones are wearing, but you do have to look professional, because it tells the world you're serious about work. This means tidy hair, natural make-up, less jewellery, and unrevealing clothes. Aim for a look that's you, but is also smart and well groomed so that you feel professional when people talk to you, and look profess-ional when people pass you in the corridors.

Utilise your contacts

You can, of course, do all of the above and still find yourself nowhere near a promotion, which is why it also pays to keep your eyes and ears open for other opportunities. You may be at the best company in the world, but if they're not recognising your worth and utilising you for it then a new less well-known company may offer you a better opportu-nity. Newspapers, headhunters and Internet job sites aside, always keep in touch with people in the same field as you, and use the tactics described above: let them know you're looking for promotion, look and act professional when they see you, aim to make an impact on them and ensure they know your USP – you never know where it will get you.

Be humble about your success

(Also known as: be gracious when you achieve success.) No one, least of all your work colleagues, wants to work

tip

To stay successful when you have achieved success is a whole other book, but you need to be prepared to work just as hard and not simply sit back and relax.

with a smug so-and-so, and no one wants to work under a power-crazed boss. When in doubt about your behaviour, always think about how you would have liked to have been treated when you were an underling, and remember: you're only as good as the last thing you did. Meaning, just because you've made it to the top it doesn't mean your job is over.

20 ways
to find job success

1 Think laterally
Stuck in a work rut? Then think outside of your current box. Instead of thinking of ways to make your job work for you, think of a new job in a new field, a new career entirely, or a side step in your company. Plenty of people move jobs within a company – and it could be the answer to your work woes if you brainstorm it clearly and properly.

2 Don't let setbacks set you back
Setbacks, although annoying and depressing, are just steep learning curves. Use them as a means to learn by focusing on what went wrong in a positive way. For example, if you didn't get a promotion, ask your immediate boss where you might have gone wrong and what you could have done differently. If you didn't get a job you were after, don't be afraid to call up human resources and ask why.

3 Avoid being ruthless
Ruthlessness is just another word for unscrupulous behaviour and it has a way of rebounding on you,

especially in work situations, so avoid stepping on others, stealing ideas and generally acting like a secret double agent just to get a few more brownie points with your boss.

4 Find a headhunter

Sometimes you can do all of the above and more, and still a company won't notice your amazing qualities and skills. If that happens, don't stick around hoping for a morsel of success to be thrown your way, see a career headhunter who will not only be brutally honest about your skills and talents but will also work their socks off to find the ideal job for you.

5 Brainstorm for success

(Also known as: put in the groundwork to find success.) Read career books, research how to get into a specific field, take courses, add skills to your portfolio and then visit a careers specialist to get more advice. You never know what you're good at and what you can really do until you've spent time thinking about it and creating a career plan.

6 Time manage yourself

Not having any time to think about where you're going in your job is the number-one complaint from people who are unhappy with their jobs. The answer is: effective time management. If you have time to take a lunch hour, time to watch breakfast TV and time to flick through magazines for new shoes, you have time to think about your career and where you want it to go.

7 Grab opportunities

How many times have you let a work opportunity slip through your fingers? If it's more than twice in the last year you need to pay closer attention to what's going on. Opportunities to grab success are more common than you think and have less to do with working all the hours God sent and more to do with volunteering for projects and presentations, and taking on jobs and roles that aren't particularly glamorous but gain you brownie points.

8 Rewrite your CV

You'd be amazed at how many people miss vital information off their CV, don't check for spelling and grammar mistakes, and generally fill their CVs with superfluous information that has nothing to do with their work. If you haven't dusted off your CV for years, it pays to invest time on it and then generally update it every three months so that when you do need to send it off you aren't scrabbling around for information and are ready to go.

9 Work on your interview style

If you haven't had an interview for a while, try to role-play a scenario with a friend who's either had a lot of interviews herself or gives interviews, as it's important to perfect your style, note how you come across to others and work on building rapport with the person interviewing you. The way to do this is to listen as much as you talk, make eye contact when listening and acknowledge the things that are being said to you.

10 Don't let work consume you

If you're working 12 hours a day, logging up overtime and forgoing your holidays in the hope you'll get noticed by your boss, bear in mind this is not an effective route to success. Firstly, it suggests that you can't get your work done in the set hours, and secondly, that you are too work-focused and may be at risk of burnout. Remember: companies like to employ individuals who have a life outside work, something you also owe yourself.

11 Prioritise what you want

(As in: know what's more important to you.) Whether it's a job title, more money, less stress or access to a new career, work on going after it. Prioritising what you want in terms of your career is essential because it's impossible to achieve everything at once. The metaphor of climbing a ladder is perfect because every rung should be a step up that you're eager to grab on to.

12 Be persistent

Persistence pays when it comes to success. Read any biography of any famous businessperson or entrepreneur and you'll see that they persevered when things went wrong and persisted even though they were turned down repeatedly. When in doubt remember J.K. Rowling who had her world-famous book *Harry Potter* rejected time and time again before it was bought up and became a hit.

13 Don't compromise your integrity

We all have morals, standards and scruples when it comes to our personal lives, and these should cross over into your working life if you want to end up happily successful (rather than just successful). Which is why it always pays to be authentic (as in: stick to what you believe in no matter what you're being offered, and don't go against your true nature).

14 Sort out your attitude

What's a bad attitude? It's an attitude that basically blames other people for your lack of success, complains rather than finds solutions and generally acts negatively when faced with a challenge. The other downside of a bad attitude is that it will never get you promoted. Think about it: would you want to work with someone who was always looking on the downside?

15 Set a time limit

It's good to have a long-term plan to reach what you're classing as success. However, it pays to set a time limit for yourself so that five years down the line you're not still at square one trying to be a pop star/actress/ business-woman. Time limits aren't there just to stop you wasting your life on something that time has shown is now unlikely to happen but are also there to help you redefine your objectives.

16 Pick your battles

Office life is a pain in the butt at times, but be wary of what battles you fight and why. Apart from being viewed as a troublemaker, if you argue every point it's a stressful way to live. Pick your battles wisely and win the war!

17 Be willing to learn from others

It's always easy to see all your bosses and managers as idiots who know nothing, but if you're open to their ways of working, and willing to learn something from everyone you meet, you'll be amazed at how your profile goes up at work and also what you do, in fact, learn.

18 Find the fun

Even the most boring workday can have an element of fun in it and it's up to you to find it, if not for your sanity then to help you to see that working can actually be a pleasurable experience. If you can't find fun in what you do, then success is never going to have the impact you want it to have.

19 Get on with people

As far as possible keep people on your side by being a pleasant person to work with, so that they always say nice things about you. In terms of job success this is vital, because you never know where you'll end up working and with whom, and also who might say a good word about you that will ensure you get that lucky lift up the ladder.

20 Enjoy the journey

Finally, you've probably heard it said a hundred times but don't just be success-orientated and always look beyond what you have. The journey to the top should be as interesting, fun and worthwhile as reaching the summit, otherwise what are you doing it for?

chapter three

Love
success

When it comes to having a successful life, love and relationship success features highly in the mix, but you're probably thinking how can you affect your love life when it's all down to luck and fate? Well, like success in any area of your life, what you believe, how you behave and what you do to get what you want tend to have a massive effect on the outcome. Sit back each night and wait for love to come knocking, or stay with someone who makes you unhappy, and your love life is guaranteed to be unsuccessful. Which means it pays to be proactive not only in your social life but also in how you think about relationships, and determine what you want from them. Like any form of success, what equals love success for you is determined by you, not the outside world, your parents or what your friends say.

Where are you now?

So let's start at the beginning: once upon a time most of us grew up dreaming of Prince Charming coming to the rescue on his white horse. Meaning, we all thought that by the time we were heading to the wrong part of our twenties we would have either the white wedding, the gorgeous (and rich) man and a baby on the way or a successful variation of all three. If you're currently single or facing some kind of relationship distress, and way past the age you thought you'd be while still at this stage, it's likely that not only has that dream retreated into the dark recesses of your mind but also your definition of love success has changed somewhat.

The good news is that, despite how you might feel, studies show that being a single woman doesn't mean you're guaranteed to be a lonely and pathetic figure who can't get by without a man at her side. Not only do surveys constantly show that most single women have great social lives, decent jobs and get out there and pursue their dreams but also that they like their lives. Which means love success is the cherry on the cake! If you're hoping it's going to be more than that and your love failures are ruining your whole life, your first step in finding love success is to get your desire for a man in perspective. Falling in love won't make your life perfect, sort out all your problems, make you successful in your career and create financial stability if you're not heading that way already. Pinning all your hopes on a man for a happy ever after is a guaranteed way to have him running for the hills, because, let's face it, who wants and needs that pressure? Fall in love because you absolutely adore, respect and admire the man you're with and because he feels the same way about you, and love success is yours.

If you're currently in a relationship, and love success still feels a great distance off, don't give up. Not all relationships run smoothly, and falling into the trap of thinking things would be easy if your love was right only leads to disaster and doom. Whereas in some cases endless arguments and a lack of communication do indicate that you'd be better off alone, in many cases making love work for you is simply about learning how to be in a relationship, because, contrary to popular belief, it's not second nature to know how to live, eat and sleep with, and love someone, 24 hours a day without sometimes being cranky, irritable and downright awkward!

What love success means

In a nutshell, love success has as much to do with who you are and what you want from life, as it does with who you meet and who you accept into your life. The good part being that no matter how stinky and rubbish your last love affair was (or the one before that, or the one before that), what counts is what happens now. So the next time you have a fight and lock yourself in the bathroom all night or find yourself on a date thinking, 'What the hell am I doing here?', remind yourself that your love success could be just round the corner. You never know.

All my single friends think you meet Mr Right and everything's OK after that. They don't realise it's hard work being with someone, making it work, and generally having to choose your arguments wisely so that every day is not a battle. I don't think anyone realises that long-term relationships are like that. **)**

Emma, 27

Don't believe the hype about your love life

Of course, when your love life stinks, one of the biggest hurdles to get over is the idea that you can't get a decent date/hold down a relationship/find love/find happiness because you're too picky, or you're too career focused, or you're unrealistic (choose the appropriate slur). However, the fact is, if your love life is in tatters or near to it, diagnosis from people outside your relationship is a waste of time, as (a) it's rarely correct; (b) it tends to come from their own agendas; and (c) all it does is reinforce beliefs that everything's gone wrong because of you.

If that rings a familiar bell, you need to remember that in this world there are crazy, annoying, lying and generally confused men who mess up relationships quite happily on their own without your help. Meaning, it's not always your fault (although sometimes you do have to take the blame and learn by your mistakes). Also, outside circumstances also affect how people behave in relationships, which

tip

If you're not going to be picky and fussy about the person you spend the whole of your life with, what *are* you going to be choosy about?

means that sometimes it's no one's fault that things go wrong. The moral of this tale is: don't listen to others; instead, work out for yourself what's happening and why, and above all, whether you're single or in a relationship that's going wrong, don't believe the hype, because it just makes eventual love success even harder.

Myths to bust include:

Myth 1: all single women are desperate to find a mate

There's a massive difference between being open to finding a new boyfriend and being obsessed with finding love. Some 99.9 per cent of single women don't fit the definition of the desperate single female, which, let's face it, hints at being a fraught and semi-hysterical woman tearing at the trouser legs of any passing male. For starters all 'single' means is 'not dating anyone'. It doesn't mean 'desperate to date anyone'. In fact one study of single women in America found that a surprising number of single girls said they had no desire to date at all, and 14 per cent said that whereas they'd date the right guy if he came along, they weren't going to knock themselves out trying to find him! Of course, there are factors that might drive you to want to find a man quicker than most, such as your age and desire to have a baby, but – and this is a big BUT – if that's your aim, the chances of you being desperate – that is, willing – to take on anyone will be even less likely.

Myth 2: single women are alone and lonely

Look up single in the dictionary and it doesn't say 'alone, lonely, miserable and sad'. The reality is these emotions can happen to anyone, even the most annoying loved-up person. So if you think you'll never feel lonely again when you fall in love, sorry but you're in for a disappointment! Whereas living alone can be lonely, especially when you can't sleep at 2.00 a.m., or your neighbours are annoying you, or your roof caves in, on the whole there is joy to be had in having your own space. Apart from sole use of the remote control, you can have the whole bed to yourself, get up when you want, sleep when you choose to and you'll never have to pick up anyone else's underpants from the floor. What's more, the huge majority of single women aren't alone, because they have a network of friends around them, plus they are more likely to have a full social life than their 'married counterparts.

'I always want to scream, "I'm single not desperate"— all my friends and family assume I sit at home every night watching TV and crying.'

Tina, 25

Myth 3: if your relationship was right you wouldn't fight

Do you fight with your mum, your best friend, and your boss? Do your siblings annoy you? Do you find yourself getting cranky even with your dog? If so, it's hardly surprising you fight with your boyfriend, because, when it comes down to it, put any two people together and eventually they'll bicker and argue. Having said that, the degree to which you fight and throw things at each other needs to be gauged. If you love and adore the person you're with but they drive you crazy on an hourly basis and this causes much friction and irritability, then you need to address the way you communicate with each other. If you fight like cat and dog and are no longer sure if you love and adore each other, then that does tend to indicate things aren't right between you. Also define the word 'fight' before you pack your bags. One relationship's endless bickering (which tends to indicate a communication problem) is another person's coming to blows (this definitely indicates you aren't in the right relationship).

tip

Don't let your birthdays define where you are in the love stakes, or other people's interpretations of when you should be in the relationship stakes.

Myth 4: you'll know instantly when it's the real thing

Ah, the great myth about eyes connecting across a room, and love happening at first sight. Whereas some women swear this happened to them, it tends to be a rewriting of history that helps this story do the rounds. Whereas there is like at first sight, and even lust at first sight, believing you'll know instantly when you see your Mr Right is a good way to avoid all the potential Mr Rights out there – in other words: a good way to avoid having a relationship. Romantic thinking like 'the one' and 'love at first sight' is the enemy of love because it makes us think that there is only one road to a relationship. Think of all the people who were friends for years before realising they were meant to be together, or the people who loathed each other on first sight and then fell in love. Don't be fooled, love can happen anywhere and with anyone, but rarely at first sight.

Myth 5: if I don't meet someone soon I'll have missed the boat

There is no age restriction when it comes to meeting some-one and falling in love, and people literally do it all the time and at any age. Yes, the pool of potential men is larger when you're in your twenties and early thirties but by the end of the thirties you get what's known as the second wave: men who are divorced, so you never truly get to the stage where all the good men have been taken. Thinking that you've somehow missed the love boat leads to giving up and so avoiding the very social situations where you could in fact meet someone.

Myth 6: you're too fussy/picky about men

You're about to break off a relationship and you're told your problem is that you're too picky. Or you hate your twentieth date in a row and someone informs you you're being too fussy. Well, if you're not going to be picky and fussy about the person you spend the whole of your life with what *are* you going to be choosy about? Whereas there are some things that indicate you're being too particular (such as you ditch him because he has the wrong colour eyes, or you don't like his name), do let your gut instinct guide you when it comes to your dates. Be fussy, be picky and be as particular as you like (within reason), and you're more likely to end up with a winner.

tip

Get love in perspective. It's wonderful but it's not everything!

What's holding you back from love success?

Your next step, whether you're single or unhappily attached, is to work out what's holding you back from love success. From the lists below tick all the answers that apply to you.

(a) If you're in an unhappy relationship, the reasons you are you staying are:

1. You believe you can still work things out.

2. You don't want to be single again.

3. This is better than nothing.

4. You know people who are worse off than you.

(b) If you're single, the reasons you have remained single are:

1. You haven't yet met the right man.

2. You never go on dates.

3. You think one day it will just happen.

4. It's better than the hassle of dealing with a man.

The correct answer for each question is 1.

If you're staying in a bad relationship because you can't face being single again or that you believe it's better to be unhappy with someone than happy alone, you're deluding yourself. Apart from whittling away your self-confidence you're wasting your time and someone else's. Like staying in a job that you hate, being in a relationship where you fight all the time, or belittle each other or even plain hate each other, just leads to an eventual acrimonious break-up, a longer period of recovery and often bitterness and regret that can seep into your next relationship.

If you're single because you haven't yet met someone, ask yourself if you're actively trying; that is, grabbing all social situations and letting it be known you're looking? Or does it mean you're being passive; that is, secretly hoping that one day you will bump into someone you like and so avoid going on dates?

Whatever is holding you back, if you're aiming for love success be honest with yourself about what you want and why, and then list all the reasons why you think you're not getting what you want. The trick with this list is to be brutally honest with yourself, it's a tough thing to do but it's instant therapy and can often help you to see something clearly that's been bothering you for months. Ask yourself:

- What am I not being honest about here?

- What am I doing wrong/what am I doing right?

- What could I change about my behaviour?

- What can't I change?

- What's the hardest thing I have to accept here?

- What's the right thing for me to do?

- What's the best way for me to do it?

- If I don't do it what's likely to happen?

You're holding yourself back from love success if you:

- Secretly want more than you have now but are afraid to admit it.
- Stay where you are in life because you're afraid to be disappointed if you try something new.
- Tell people you're happy being single/attached but you know you're not.
- Feel jealousy and envy when someone you know finds love success.
- Don't believe love success can happen to you.

Looking at yourself and your relationship

Introspection is good, over-analysis is not. So to make a good relationship strong ensure you put energy into being and staying together. Here's how:

Step 1: know what you want when you're in a relationship

Knowing what you *don't* want is one thing, but knowing what you *do* want is another thing entirely, because when it comes to relationships it pays to be specific. This means that if you're in relationship distress you need to work out what it is you want from your current relationship. Ask yourself:

- What do I want to change?

- What do I need to change about my behaviour?

- What do I want my partner to do?

- What does he want me to do?

- What's making me unhappy?

- How could I improve this situation?

- Is this relationship a lost cause, and if not, what's giving me hope?

Step 2: improve the way you communicate

In an ideal world we'd talk lovingly and respectfully to each other at all times, but as anyone who's been in a relation-ship knows, that's hard to do when you love someone, never mind when you're going through a rough patch with them. The way you speak to each other, however, affects a lot of things in your relationship and also tends to indicate levels of respect. Meaning, if you want a relationship where the other person respects and listens to you, you need to

work out how to communicate this effectively. If you're unsure of whether someone respects you, look at how he talks to you. Talking over someone, ignoring what they say and generally putting them down shows arrogance and selfishness, not love. Likewise, constant bickering hints at the fact that important issues are being ignored between the two of you; that is, instead of fighting about the washing-up are you really fighting about who takes who for granted? Not listening is something we're all guilty of, but if you're doing it constantly is it because you're no longer interested in what your partner has to say or have you just forgotten how to be interested in each other?

Key question Write down five ways that would improve the way you communicate with each other.

Step 3: think about where you're heading together

When you got together you were probably thinking about where you were heading, or you might not have thought about it at all, which is why this area needs to be addressed regularly, as it changes as you get older and as your life circumstances change. Focus on it at least twice a year so that you don't wake up one day assuming this was going to lead to marriage and kids, and find out that wasn't what your boyfriend was thinking. It's also easy to ascertain what someone's future relationship goals are without having to have deep and meaningful conversations all the time. Look at how he treats you, and how he talks about your future (are you mentioned in it or does he seek your opinion about it?) and how he responds when you talk about yours. Is he interested in where you want to go and why, or is he quick to avoid the subject? If you get a strong gut feeling that the person you're with has different aspirations to you, discuss it with him. Be 100 per cent clear about what he's saying and then decide if it's something you want or not.

Key question Write down your future goals, his future goals and whether you have any future goals as a couple (look for crossover goals).

Step 4: are you still compatible?

Working out if your personalities match is a hard one. 'Opposites attract', say some people, and they do, but only if there are underlying compatibilities, such as you both want the same thing, you both have similar backgrounds, and you're both heading the same way. That's not to say you can't make it if you have wildly differing traits, but it is harder and you do have to be more accommodating, especially if you had a checklist of what you felt you wanted from a boyfriend and your boyfriend doesn't match up (this works both ways).

Another problem with personalities is that we all change

(due to life circumstances, your partner's job or even simply growing older), and because when we first fall in love we tend to idealise the person we fall in love with, most of us are reluctant to accept this change and move with the times. If you feel that way you need to look at what kind of person you want to be with and why. And then ask yourself whether you feel threatened by your partner changing. Or were you hoping to change someone and it hasn't worked, or is someone trying to change you?

Key question Do you still like and admire your boyfriend and does he feel the same way about you? If not, why are you still hanging around?

Knowing what you want when you're single

When it comes to knowing who you want, perhaps you have a list as long as your arm filled with his personality traits (must have a sense of humour, be smart and know how to count), your financial wants (must earn over 100k a year) and his physical attributes (tall, dark hair) – or maybe all you want is a man with a pulse! Whatever traits you desire, knowing what you want when you're single will determine your success level at meeting someone. Having said that, choosing is a delicate game of balance between who you think your ideal man should be, and who in reality he might be. Take on anyone and try him on for size and you risk date fatigue, be list obsessed and you may never get a date. To help you pinpoint what you want and why, consider the following:

Step 1: what's on your checklist?

If you have a list in your head of attributes that your ideal partner would possess, you're not alone. Whereas it can be fun to speculate who we might end up with and who we'd like to end up with, a checklist can actually stop you from dating. Being fixated on someone looking or being a certain way is ridiculous for many reasons. Firstly, you're not ordering a pizza with different toppings, you're talking about meeting someone who is real and multilayered. Secondly, think how insulting it would be if someone turned you down because you fit only two out of his five must-have points, and thirdly, how likely are you to ever meet someone who fulfils 90 per cent of your list?

If you're still not convinced, take a look at your list and consider how many of the elements you possess yourself. Is it really fair, for example, to expect Mr Right to be fit if you haven't done any exercise since you donned PE knickers at school? Or is it fair to want him to have a car/house or earnings of 100k a year when you have none of these things? If 60 per cent of your list is made up of things that you don't possess you're really looking for a lifestyle not a man.

On the other hand, if you have absolutely no idea of who you're looking for and why, you're at risk of never knowing when you do meet your Mr Right. Like looking for ideal shoes or the right job, you need to have a loose idea of what you're looking for. Think of traits you admire in your friends and yourself, and where you feel your future lies, and that will help you to have a vague idea of what you want and why.

Key question Is your checklist helping or hindering your dating life?

Step 2: what do you want from a relationship?

As well as knowing what you want from a partner, it's also essential to know what you want from a relationship and what you expect it to bring to your life. The problem many single people have is that they assume being in love will solve all their problems, so they imagine that once they're hooked up with someone they'll never feel lonely, unhappy or depressed again. Which is why it's vital to remember that whereas a relationship can bring you many things it doesn't have the power to make your life perfect.

When considering what you want from a lover think about what you're looking for before you pair up with

tip

Dating is a numbers game – you have to get out there and meet as many people as you can, so you have a higher chance of meeting someone you will really get on with.

someone, because it's the fundamental wants that will determine your relationship's success potential with someone – and, contrary to popular belief, we're not all looking for the same thing. So ask yourself, are you looking for:

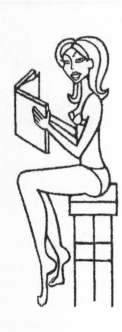

- Commitment?

- Fidelity?

- Potential marriage down the line?

- To have a child down the line?

- An open relationship?

- To live with someone?

- To live apart?

- To settle down?

- To live it up?

Key question What fundamental needs weren't fulfilled in your previous relationships?

Step 3: are you dating?

This seems like a crazy question to ask in a chapter about love success, but the fact is that sometimes women forget that they're not actually dating because they spend so much time talking and thinking about being single and meeting someone. The key advice when it comes to love success is less talking, more dating. More dating doesn't mean date anyone but take a pick-and-mix attitude to your dates. Try out men you wouldn't usually consider if you feel a spark there, challenge your prejudices about different types of men and, like trying on a variety of clothes, give different guys a chance to see if you're right or wrong. Why? Well, believe it or not, it's often the elements we haven't thought about that make us connect with someone, and often these factors that create a deeper relationship.

Key question How many dates have you been on in the last year (aim for four to six, at least, a year)?

How to date more successfully

It's all very well telling you to get out there and get a date, but the number-one question on your lips is probably: how do I get one? The answer is you need to get out there and meet as many people as you can, and not necessarily in bars and clubs if that's not your thing. Go to places where you like to hang out because that's where you're going to meet someone compatible, such as the coffee shop, the gym or the cinema (though obviously you'll probably have to join a cinema club rather than try to pick up someone in the dark during a screening!).

Next, you have to flirt – that is, send out signals that (a) you're single; and (b) you're looking. Sit back and keep your head down, or always head out with a bunch of girl-friends and all that will happen is people will assume you're attached. Lastly, you have to tell people you're single and, contrary to popular belief, it's not desperate to tell people you're looking to date or to say you're single. If you think it is, bear in mind that it's the proactive that end up winning the dating game, not the girls who sit back and complain that there are no decent men out there or wait for fate to step in.

Finally, the last thing you need to know about successful dating is it's supposed to be fun. Yes, it's nerve-racking and anxiety-ridden and, yes, sometimes it can be downright demoralising, but on the whole when you go out you should be aiming to have fun with the person you're with, or else why are you bothering?

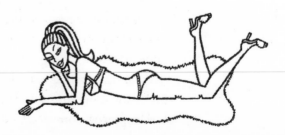

> ## The unsuccessful lazy girl way to date:
>
> - Spend all your time whining about being single.
> - Date like a mad woman.
> - Instantly tell your dates your dating history.
> - Instantly tell your dates you're looking for marriage.
> - Tell your date about your checklist.
> - Think sex seals the deal.
> - Spend all your time scanning dating sites.
> - Give up after one date.
> - Convince yourself it will just happen one day.
> - Convince yourself you're undatable!

How to find love

Ask yourself where you've found love before. The answer will help you to see that you can find dates anywhere – at the gym, on the bus, even at the supermarket. Of course, as life changes so do our chances of meeting single people, which is why after a certain age you may find that your old sources of dates have dried up. If this is the case, don't give up. Sometimes you have to think outside of the box to win, even if the outside part feels scary and somewhat desperate. Here's what you need to know:

1. Where you look tends to determine your outcome

Go to an online dating site or via a dating agency or any-where that people pay money to find dates (speed dating, dinner clubs) and you're likely to find people who are seri-ous about finding love, as opposed to going to a bar where people are more likely to be looking for a one-night stand. However, contrary to popular belief, going through a paid intermediary to find love is not the domain of the desper-ate and lonely. Many people are on sites and at agencies because their social circle has shrunk and they no longer have opportunities to find dates, or they live in an area where they don't know many people. If you think you're scraping the bottom of the barrel by doing Internet dating you shouldn't try these sites because you're going in with the wrong attitude (and an insulting one) and are unlikely to find a date.

The reality is there has been a 7 per cent increase in online dating in the last year alone, with more than 5 mil-lion people logging in daily to find love, because they know online sites tend to work much better than traditional dating agencies (which tend to be more age specific, and definitely more pricey). Better still, with Internet dating you can do it in private, find someone who is much more your age, see a picture before you choose and generally meet someone with similar interests to you.

Of course the stigma of Internet dating sites, agencies

and adverts still exists because many people wrongly believe that attractive people don't need to 'look' for love in this way so the sites and adverts must be full of 'losers'. The reality is they're full of people looking for love and being proactive about it, and if you give them a try you'll be surprised by what you might find there.

Lazy girl good places to find a date:

- At work (not necessarily your department).
- Through friends and friends of friends.
- Coffee shops at night or weekend mornings.
- Anywhere you frequent a lot.
- At an evening class.
- On a long-distance journey.
- Through your friends' boyfriends.
- Through a work event.

The other place to look is around you, because finding someone in your world is the best way to find someone compatible. Who are you missing in your daily life? Is work really a single-man-free zone? Do your friends really know no one good they can set you up with? Is there no man who crosses your path regularly that you like? Open your eyes and look around you critically. Ask friends for blind dates, check your parents' friends' kids – and don't look elsewhere until you've left every stone unturned.

2. *You have to flirt*

Flirting has had a bit of a bad rap of late because people assume if you're a 'flirt' it means you're a bit flighty and manipulative, but this isn't the case. Flirting is about understanding and making the most of your verbal and non-verbal signals so that you can attract someone or let them know you like them; that is, it's about being charming. We all do it in everyday life whether we realise it or not, because even though we put so much emphasis on what we say, we actually spend more time unconsciously reading other people's non-verbal signals (that is, their body language and tone of voice). In the dating world this is emphasised even more by the fact that we're all on the lookout for 'signs' that someone likes us.

To send out your own signs it helps to believe you're someone who is worth getting to know, because the power of flirting lies in projecting positive messages about yourself so that the person you're flirting with gets the message that you're fun and good to be around. Giggling or staring blankly when a man smiles at you aren't hot flirt moves, neither is being rude to someone who asks you out just because you don't like him, or being over the top with someone when you do. The trick is to:

- Smile and be friendly when you spot someone you like.

- Go over and say hello if you like someone and they are smiling at you.

- Don't be sexually OTT, instead ask questions to see if you have stuff in common.

- Check out their body language to see if their smile reaches their eyes when they look at you (fake smiles don't), and if they move closer or further away from you when you speak (moving away means either you're too close or they're not interested).

- Trust your gut instinct to see if they like you.

- Don't overstay your welcome, especially if they're with friends, and especially if they try to wind things up.

- Don't sink into a depression if you get turned down; think onwards and upwards and try again. Just as you don't like everyone who flirts with you, not everyone you approach will be open to you.

3. You have to be sure you're with someone you like

You've found a man, you like him and he likes you. Questions to ask yourself before throwing yourself in at the deep end are:

Is he single?

If you've met this man at a bar, or through an Internet site or advert it's worth checking out if he is indeed single. You'd be amazed at how many men try it on.

Does he want a relationship?

If he's saying he's not sure, or he's still living with his ex, or he's about emigrate, he doesn't want a relationship. Be realistic – it will save you from a broken heart.

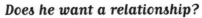

Is he on the same page as you?

Meaning, does he want the same things as you (see Step two: what do you want from a relationship? on page 87) and if not, is he someone worth investing time in?

Are there definite things going against the two of you?

Such as he lives 200 miles away or in a different country, or he has very different religious or moral beliefs from you? While you can overcome some of these things, if you don't address them they can tear you apart.

Is he a nice person?

Of course he's being nice to you because you've just met him and he's trying to impress you, but watch for his behaviour around his friends and work colleagues. Also, look how he treats waiters, shop assistants and people you come across. How he treats others will give you a clear indication of how one day he'll treat you.

Do you really like him?

Or have you been flattered into dating him? Or persuaded into it by friends, or even convinced yourself that he's the one because no one else is on the scene? The way to determine this is simple: if you want to spend time with him over everything else, you really like him; if a soap opera or a night in washing your hair is tempting you away, you don't!

20 ways
to love success

1 Like yourself
It sounds weird, but if you want someone else to like you, you've got to like yourself first, otherwise you'll always wonder what it is they like about you, and so doubt their love. Boost your self-esteem by learning to like and appreciate who you are, rather than wait to be validated by another person.

2 Communicate effectively
The problem with communication is that we always assume we are making ourselves crystal-clear and are saying what we want, but if your partner is always confused by you or says he doesn't understand what's going on, you need to improve your verbal and listening skills. Limit misunderstandings by repeating back what you've heard in important conversations and reiterating what you say.

3 Be honest with yourself and others

(As in: be honest about what you want and what you're looking for, and be honest about what's going wrong.) It's no good pretending things are OK or saying you don't want commitment, when you're dreaming of a white wedding and naming your, as yet, unborn children, or pretending you're happy being single because you can't face dating!

4 Have fun

That's have fun whether you're single or attached, because that's the whole point of love or life. If you're not having fun then something is not right – and it's up to you to work it out.

5 Play the field and then choose

Forget waiting for one perfect man – if you're looking to be happy in love you have to try on lots of different types of men to see what suits you and what doesn't. So play the field, but in the end choose someone (in other words, don't get addicted to just dating).

6 Don't expect perfection

That's perfection in a partner, perfection in a relationship and even perfection in yourself! Love and life are messy, and you have to accept that nothing's perfect all the time. If you hang about waiting for it you could well wake up alone.

7 Work through the hard times

It's easy to run for the hills when relationships get hard, and while sometimes this is the right thing to do, anything worth having is worth fighting tooth and nail for. So make sure you work hard to make love work and if it's still broken then that's the time to leave, and not before.

8 Be kind

If you're dating, there are going to be times when you meet the wrong man, and/or get asked out by some- one you consider to be three levels beneath you. When this happens, be kind because (a) you never know when the tables will be turned; and (b) even if you don't like someone, it's a compliment to be asked out, and the person deserves you at least to be polite in your rejection of them.

9 Sell yourself

Dating is a game of self-promotion, which means when you're on a date it pays to sell yourself; that is, tell him you're great (within reason), because if you don't who will? Don't be the woman who lists all her bad points and explains why the last ten men left her!

10 Don't idolise men

It's easy when you've been single for a while to imagine all men are wonderful, perfect creatures, and the reason you're single is because you're not worthy. This is rubbish – men aren't perfect. They are like you and me, and if you idolise them, all you're doing is setting yourself up for failure when they fall off the pedestal you've put them on.

11 Don't demonise men

Likewise, not all men are lying, deceiving cheats who use women just for sex. If you've had a bad run of dates or a bad relationship it can be easy to demonise men, but bear in mind all you're doing is making the chances of love success harder for yourself. Not all men are bad, just as not all women are good!

12 Look at your beliefs about relationships

For true love success you need to analyse your beliefs about what equals a good relationship and diagnose whether you're helping or hindering yourself. Are you someone who believes in Happily Ever After or someone who considers that all men want to cheat even when they're in love? Are your beliefs based on reality or myth?

13 Being single isn't a failure

... just as being married doesn't mean you're a love success. What matters is how you view your life. Being single isn't a failure if you've chosen to wait until you meet the right man, and are living your life the way you want. Don't let other people determine whether you're a success or not!

14 Don't give up

(As in: it's never too late to find or fall in love.) This means don't give up, because if you're looking, one day you'll find it. Why? Well, because it's a numbers game and if you date wide and far, eventually you will find your Mr Right and you will get the relationship you want.

15 Don't overdate

There's nothing more likely to have you reaching for the remote control every night than going through a phase of dating like a mad woman. Trying out different forms of dating, going on blind dates and being proactive is one thing, but making yourself date every week for the sake of it is another. Overdating means date burnout!

16 Remember your other relationships
Love success is not just about your relationships with men, so whether you're in a relationship or not, don't forget about putting some time and attention into all your other relationships – especially friends and family.

17 Focus on the present and future, not the past
The great majority of us have a terrible past record with men and love, which is why it doesn't pay to focus on your past, but your present and future. Yes, you can learn from what happened, but every relationship is different, and beating yourself up about the past does nothing but keep you there.

18 Re-evaluate your relationship every six months
Whether it's going well or not, for the sake of love success it pays to look at your relationship every six months and work out what could be improved, what might be going wrong and what you need to improve on.

19 Love is all around you
Corny but true – if you look around and everyone

else seems to be in love and loved up, don't be demoralised by it, but be motivated by it. If it can happen to all those people, it can, and will, happen to you.

20 Remember: success can be yours

If you're feeling despondent and fed up about love, don't despair – you never know what's around the corner if you make the effort to look!

chapter four

Financial
success

tip

Are you suffering from the lazy girl's financial success strategy, which entails either winning the lottery, marrying a multimillionaire, and/or suddenly waking up and being offered a massive pay rise/bonus? Or do you imagine that one day all your financial problems will just be solved because you'll inherit an immense amount of wealth from a relative you never knew existed? If so, you're not alone in your financial fantasising, but, sadly, in the real world if you're seriously looking for financial success you've got to do more than dream big, live on an overdraft and use your credit cards to survive on. You need to have a plan, and a plan means getting serious about your cash flow, not throwing your bank statements unopened into the bin and not putting endless things on your credit card because you have a classic buy-now-pay-tomorrow attitude.

Now for the good news: just because you have zero savings, a large debt and a low income it doesn't mean you can't one day be financially successful, as in being wealthier than you are now and with less debt and fewer sleepless nights over your lack of cash. Financial security can be yours even if you're the laziest girl around, with just a few simple changes in your spending, budgeting and saving. If all those words send you to sleep, you need to think about where you want to be in ten years' time, because the truth is how you spend/save your money today directly influences how you will live tomorrow. Which means apart from Prince Charming rushing in and saving you in his Aston Martin, the decision about whether you are poorer or richer in your future lies in your hands, and your hands alone!

You can still find financial success lazy girl style if:

- You're in debt.
- You're on a low wage.
- You're useless with money.
- You're a spendaholic.
- You're rubbish at keeping accounts.
- You spend more than you earn.
- You can't add up.
- You don't understand accounting.

As long as you ...

- Are open to learning.
- Work out a debt repayment plan and stick to it.
- Write down everything you spend.
- Spend less than you earn.
- Budget even when you're solvent.
- Make short-term and long-term investments.
- Utilise your earning skills.
- Think before you spend.
- Think about why you spend.

Are you useless with money?

❛ I'm someone who's useless with money. I never know how much I have in my account, I feel nervous when I use the ATM machine and at the end of the month I am always overdrawn and can't make my credit card payments. ❜

Sam, 24

There are, of course, very few lazy girls (or, let's face it, people in general) who love budgeting and not spending money, so if you're someone who knows they could be financially more on the case then you really aren't alone. However, having said that, never knowing how much is in your account, feeling nervous every time you put your ATM card in the machine and being scared of your bank statements tends to indicate that you are lazier than most about your cash, the question is why?

Most lazy financial girls fall into the 'I'm useless with money' category, either by choice (who's got time to keep accounts and open bank statements?) or because they've been told they are useless with money, or because they failed maths a hundred years ago and imagine this makes them bad with their cash. Again, the good news is:

- If you can add and subtract (even on your fingers) and/or use a calculator, you can be good with money.

- If you can work out how to afford an amazing pair of shoes and three takeaways a week on a disappearing budget then you can be great with money.

- If you have a huge debt and you're good at juggling your money around to make all your payments each month, you can be excellent with money.

It's all about gaining a better attitude and financial confidence so that you feel you're able to (a) understand money; and (b) cope with your finances. Keep telling yourself you're rubbish and silly with your cash and that's how you'll behave. Turn over a new leaf and start educating yourself about cash, learn to budget, save and ask for help, and you'll not only feel less panic-ridden about your finances but also more in control (so fewer tearful nights). Once you feel you can handle money and not be scared of it, you'll not only learn that you can live within your means (a huge part of being financially successful) but also you will feel able to make good decisions about what you spend and save, and so find financial success for life. The way to do it is simple:

Step 1: find a money mentor

This is someone who is good with money and sensible about their spending. It pays to pick someone you (a) trust; and (b) isn't connected to your finances. It could be a friend, or a relative. This person's job is not to sort out your finances for you but to help you sort out your finances by supporting your effort to change, and showing you how to budget and work on reducing your debt. This person is your financial buddy – someone to call up when you're lacking in confidence, feeling stuck and/or feeling tempted to go back to your old ways.

Step 2: seek professional help

Whereas asking for help from the very people who scare you may seem ridiculous, people like your bank manager and/or credit card companies are there to help, and actually want to help you. So, rather than seek help from dubious sources, such as loan companies that you've never heard of or credit card companies who offer you massive loans, go right to the base source for help. Whether this is your bank manager, your credit card company, a debt helpline or a financial adviser, these people can help you sort out your financial problems once and for all, and will give you the strategies to fix your current financial problems on a long-term basis. Talk to these people about debt reduction, loan payments, savings, bonds and pensions.

Step 3: tell yourself you can do it

Anyone can learn to be good with money. You need to keep telling yourself this; otherwise, you'll never feel confident about handling your finances. Think of your money management like learning to drive – you feel nervous at first, then you get confident with the help of an instructor, but finally you have to go it alone, or else you know you'll never truly feel confident about driving. Remember: you have to be positive about your ability to go for it so that you can believe in your decisions and feel financially able. Keep reminding yourself that money management is not rocket science. It's simply about adding and subtracting, and the root equation is simple: spend less than you earn and you'll be solvent. Spend more than you earn and you'll be in debt.

tip

If you have a huge debt and you're good at juggling your money around to make all your payments each month, you can be excellent with money.

You're a spendaholic if you:

- Buy something and don't realise you already have it at home.
- Get your thrills from the buying rather than the actual product.
- Feel an adrenalin rush when you go shopping and buy something.
- Hide the amount you spend from loved ones.

- Rarely use or open the things you buy.
- Always go for three-for-two deals and sales, because you tell yourself you're really 'saving' money.
- Feel panic-ridden if you go somewhere with no shops.
- Shop online when you can't think of anything else to do.

Know your financial goals

Of course, knowing in your head what you 'should' be doing (that is, not overspending and living beyond your means) is one thing, but if you want financial success you have to know what your financial goals are. Your aim should be to pick goals that are (a) realistic; and (b) practical. Meaning, saying you want to be a millionaire and/or that you will never have to work again, although possibly achievable (with huge amounts of effort, planning and long-term action) aren't the average lazy girl's practical goals. Your goals should be based on your current financial situation and a five-year plan. Meaning, work out where you are now financially, and then where you'd like to be financially in five years' time, and your goals should then become crystal-clear to you.

For example:

Lazy girl scenario 1 If you're currently thousands in debt, with no savings, and a lifestyle that outruns your earning potential, your financial-success goals should be:

Goal 1 – to get out of debt in the shortest time possible.

Goal 2 – to up your earning potential.

Goal 3 – to learn to budget.

Lazy girl scenario 2 If you currently live from one pay cheque to the next and have no savings or spare cash, your financial success goals should be:

Goal 1 – to increase your earning potential.

Goal 2 – to start a savings plan.

Lazy girl scenario 3 If you currently have savings but no assets or investments, your goals should be:

Goal 1 – seek advice on long-term investments and assets that can start making money for you.

Goal 2 – learn how to make your money work for you.

When making your goals, think short term (a month), long term (a year) and future term (five years), and ask yourself what you would like to be different about your finances in a month's time. Possible answers to short-term goals are: you'll feel more in control of what you're doing, you'll have a budget, you'll have worked out how to make more money, you'll have cut back on spending and made sure you were saving money on everything from your bills to your rent.

Possible answers to long-term goals: you'll have less or no debt, you'll feel in total control of your finances, you'll have a little bit saved, you'll have upped your earnings and you'll be living to a budget.

Possible answers to future goals: you'll have investments such as a property, you'll have assets that make you money, you'll have a higher income, and you'll have short-term and long-term savings.

Invest in the financial-success game plan

Now you have your financial goals in place you need to get a financial game plan going, which takes into account your spending, your cash flow and a budget. This means it's time to get real and understand that the main root of many financial problems lies in the fact that a quarter of us have absolutely no idea at all about what we're spending, and more like half of us have only a limited grasp of our outgoings on a weekly or monthly basis; furthermore, one in five people don't know the balance on their current account. On top of this, under 50 per cent don't know the balance on their credit card. If you have a similar head-in-the-sand approach to your finances, it's time to wake up and smell the coffee because before you can work out where you're going you will have to take a long, hard look at where you are.

Your finances and spending need immediate taking in hand if:

- You don't have a clue how much money or debt you have.

- You don't know exactly how much you earn each month.

- You readily admit you're not in control of your money.

- When you pay with plastic, you tell yourself it's not real money.

- You use your credit card as a safety net.

- You live in fear of working out how much you owe.

- You have more than one credit card, store card and debit card.

- You have a long-term debt, an overdraft and loan.

- You only ever make minimum repayments on credit cards.

- You have no idea how much you buy each week.

fact

When using debit cards, 41 per cent of females are likely to overspend compared to 35 per cent of males, because, they say, 'psychologically it feels like I'm not spending money'.

Step 1: create a weekly and monthly budget

Know your monthly, weekly and daily budget. Yes, budget, as in draw up a daily financial plan, stick to it and believe in it! If the very word strikes the fear of God into your heart it's likely you have never budgeted and have no idea how to live within your means, and maybe even have no idea how to draw up a budget that could save your financial life. So here's how to do it. Gather together your wage slip, your bills, your bank statements, and credit and store card payments, grab a calculator and start writing:

Income per month   ⎯⎯⎯⎯⎯⎯⎯

Outgoings per month (essentials):

Mortgage/rent   ⎯⎯⎯⎯⎯⎯

Gas   ⎯⎯⎯⎯⎯⎯

Electricity   ⎯⎯⎯⎯⎯⎯

Telephone _____

Water _____

Service charge (if applicable) _____

Insurance (if applicable) _____

Council/local tax _____

Travel costs _____

Credit card/store card payments _____

Loan payments _____

Miscellaneous (other money owed) _____

Food (not socialising) _____

Home supplies (essential products) _____

Total _____

The money that's left is now the amount to budget with; that is, the money you have to live on for the month. Divide this amount by four and you'll find your weekly budget. This is the amount that you have for all your non-essentials such as socialising and spending.

If you're now laughing because the amount is paltry, or you are horrified because there's practically no money left, it indicates that either you're totally living beyond your means (look at your rent and bills) or have huge debts that are crippling you (look at your repayments). If you can do nothing about these things, then it's your budget that you have to make cutbacks in. Before you start stamping your feet and saying you can't do it, remind yourself that your goal is financial success and you're never going to get there if you refuse to change your ways and insist on living the way you do now. After all, it's your habits and behaviour now that have got you into financial deep water, so it's these you have to change, whether you like it or not.

Step 2: make cutbacks everywhere

List all your non-essentials:

Meals out (including lunches and coffees)   _____

Drinks (alcoholic)   _____

Mobile phone/Internet   _____

Books/magazines/papers   _____

Cinema/DVDs/videos/CDs   _____

Gym membership   _____

Presents   _____

Clothes   _____

Beauty and toiletries (including hair)   _____

Miscellaneous   _____

Total   _____

Ask yourself: can you go out less, buy less, live off cash not credit, take lunch to work, go to the library instead of buying books, cut out the gym membership and generally change your lifestyle for good? You may be screaming 'NO WAY', but the reality is that if you want financial success these are the tricks that get you there. And contrary to popular belief it doesn't mean a life of no fun, but a life where you accept you have only a certain amount of cash and learn to live within your means. Ways to do this are simple; for example:

tip

The root of many financial problems lies in the fact that a quarter of us have absolutely no idea at all about what we're spending.

- If you usually buy a newspaper or magazines, think about swapping with friends or viewing online, or even going to a library to read free copies.

- If you always buy a coffee and muffin on the way to work, eat breakfast at home.

- If you buy lunch and a snack every day, again, bring in some home-made lunch and a snack.

- If you buy a ready-made meal on the way home, learn to cook.

- If you get taxis everywhere, buy a travel card.

- If you have a gym membership, work out to a home video or go for a run in the park.

- If you rent DVDs from a local store, do it from your library or online where it's cheaper.

Of course, you don't have to be this radical to see savings. Just bringing in lunch each day can save you a significant amount of cash. Of course, you may think that small changes mean nothing when you owe thousands, but bear in mind that saving some money each day adds up and does save you a significant amount of cash in the long run. Of course, if cutting back drastically from your non-essentials makes little or no difference, or leaves you no money to save, you have to consider other life changes:

- Look at who you're paying and how much you're paying. Studies show people could save a heap of cash on their utility bills, for example, by shopping around for a cheaper supplier. These days it's easier to do than you think; just go to one of the many Internet companies that happily do it online for you.

- Next, count up your credit and debit cards, store cards, and other debts, such as an overdraft or catalogue balance. You need to take the money stress out of your life by reducing the number of monthly bills you have to settle. If you have, say, three credit cards, you need to switch the balances of all three on to one card with a very low interest rate – giving you a chance to get to grips with your debt.

- Get rid of your store cards. These cards have huge interest and penalty fees and they should be avoided at all costs. Cut the cards up and concentrate on paying them back.

- Look at your mobile, telephone, and Internet connection fee. Are you getting a great deal or haven't you bothered to check? Check the Internet and, while you're at it, do you know how much you're paying a year for insurance? You could save hundreds by just checking out what people are charging you and whether you even need what they're offering you.

10 ways to save about 10 per cent of your wages a month:

1. Go out only once a week to eat.
2. Eat breakfast at home.
3. Don't buy magazines or papers.
4. Don't rent DVDs.
5. Cancel your gym membership if you don't go more than once a week.
6. Only use your mobile phone for taking calls.
7. Swap books with friends.
8. Work in cash – leave your cards at home.
9. Don't shop when you're bored.
10. Go to the pub later than usual so that you drink less.

Step 3: lose the treat mentality and the 'I deserve' mentality

❛ I've got my money under control now, but I know I still have a treat mentality. I still feel the urge to buy something if I have a bad day, or treat myself to something if something good happens. ❜

Liz, 25

You have a treat mentality if you:

- Reward yourself for being good.
- Always comfort yourself with a purchase after a bad day.
- Think you deserve to have nice things because you're stressed/upset/angry.
- Always 'buy' a present for yourself when you're buying for others.
- Always buy something when you feel hard done by.
- Buy things because you're single/poor/fed up/have a hard job.

The treat mentality, or the 'I deserve' mentality, is the idea that somehow, even though you don't earn X amount, you deserve to have the life of someone who does, because (a) it's not fair that you can't afford it; and (b) you've had a hard day/life/job so you deserve it. The problem is that until you change this thought process you won't be able to change anything about your financial situation, because it's how you think about money and what you believe that determines your behaviour towards it.

The reality is if you want a certain lifestyle you can't buy it, you have to work for it, plan for it and generally delay gratification until the day when you truly have enough money to treat yourself to, say, a five-star getaway or a brand-new car or designer clothes and champagne. Until then locate where your attitude came from. The roots of what you believe you're allowed or need tend to be in childhood, so work out if you're trying to repair something from back then or simply acting *against* your background or whether you are acting *true to* your background.

If that doesn't ring true, work out why you spend. Rather like a comfort eater who needs to find out why she overeats, there are strong psychological impulses to spending and treating yourself. Are you depressed about something, or bored? When do you spend the most? At weekends or when you're down? What is it about spending that makes you feel better? The answers to these questions will help you to work out what you're doing and why, so that you can change your behaviour by recognising what you're doing before you do it (that is, giving yourself the choice not to do it).

tip

Why save now? Because time is not on your side. Your best saving years are in your twenties and thirties when your wages are on the up, and you don't yet have dependants (children) and large expenses such as a mortgage and substantial bills.

Step 4: create a repayment plan that prioritises your debts

A repayment plan is a plan that's based on paying back your debts as quickly and as methodically as possible, but that also allows you some space to live so you're not forced to exist on a pittance for five years. When you're massively in debt the idea that one day you'll be debt-free can seem about as likely as winning the lottery, but it can be done because people do it every day. All you have to remember is repayment means just that, you are repaying what you've already spent, not being punished. Financial rehab hurts, but rather than run from the pain learn from it, because it will stop you getting in debt again.

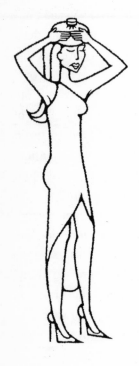

For an effective repayment plan you need to open your bills and look at what you owe. It's scary but it's only by calculating everything you owe to banks, store cards, credit cards, and friends and family that you'll have an honest figure to start from. Leave stuff out and all that will happen is your repayment plan will veer rapidly off course within a month. So start by casting a glance back over your budget and see how much you have put aside to repay your debts. Have you budgeted for only minimum repayments? If so, you need to rethink and come up with a larger figure; otherwise you'll never be debt-free.

Then start prioritising your debt. Write a list of all your debts, starting with the loan/credit card that has the

highest interest rate, rather than the loan/credit card that
has the highest debt. If all your cards hold the same interest, start by paying off the biggest loan first.

Creditors	Per cent interest	Payback amount	Debt-free date
Store card 1	_____	_____	_____
Store card 2	_____	_____	_____
Credit card 1	_____	_____	_____
Credit card 2	_____	_____	_____
Loan 1	_____	_____	_____
Loan 2	_____	_____	_____
Money owed to family	_____	_____	_____
Money owed to friends	_____	_____	_____
Car loans	_____	_____	_____
Household product loans	_____	_____	_____
Bills owed	_____	_____	_____
Overdraft	_____	_____	_____

When paying off your debts:

- Contact your creditors if you're having problems paying off your debts. They will stop sending you threatening letters and work out a payment plan for you.

- Make sure that you always make your payments on time, as all banks and credit companies have late fees that click in after even one day.

- Cut up the cards that you're paying back so that you're not tempted to keep spending.

- Only use cash to pay for things (not debit cards/store cards or credit cards) so that you can see exactly how much you're spending.

- Direct-debit your repayments to come out of your account on the day you're paid, to ensure the payments definitely happen each month.

- Contact a debt helpline (NOT a debt company that offers you more loans) if you're in dire straits (see Resources).

- If you're consolidating your debt (that is, getting a loan to cover it all and then paying back the loan) read the small print before you sign, and only go to reputable sources. Pay attention to the loan rate and look to see how much you pay back overall.

Save, Save, Save

Warning! If you're struggling to pay off debts and survive on your budget, you're not ready to invest and start saving. What's more if you're £20,000 in debt it's totally pointless to have a few thousand saved. The interest on your debts far outweighs the interest you're reaping from your savings, so think about using some of the money to pay off a credit card and cancel your debts. On the other hand if you have some spare cash lying about and you haven't had a savings account since you were a little girl and saved in a piggy bank, it's time to get serious about savings; and by spare cash I'm talking about excess cash that you usually just fritter away on tat (tat is all that stuff you buy but don't need or rarely use).

'Why bother?' you might think, especially if you have no extra money, or don't like to live for the future. Well, savings have a dual role: on the one hand it pays to have some money stored up for if you want to go on holiday, buy a house, or one day get married and have kids, because these expenses all cost, and cost big. This means that even if you don't have the whole amount, a little bit of money saved can act as a fairly good deposit. Also, whereas it's easy to go through life and imagine your income will keep going up and you'll never be out of a job, you don't know what's round the corner, and if the worst does occur what will you live off if you have no savings? Hard times are just one reason why money experts suggest that a sign of being financially successful is having at least two months' wages saved so that if the worst does occur you have money for rent, food and bills. If that sounds unlikely or impossible for you, then save smaller; every little bit helps and every little bit grows, especially if you leave it untouched for a number of years.

On top of this, if you get satisfaction out of buying and shopping, and having things, it might help to know that having savings is rewarding, in more ways than one. Seeing your money accumulate, and watching your balance go up and up and up, is strangely exhilarating. And once you have a certain amount stored away it's somewhat thrilling to know that you have a nice little cushion should a rainy day come.

If you've always been too lazy to save, the key is to have saving goals that are long term (for when you're old), short term (holidays and Christmas) and mid term (a house, a wedding, a baby). Long term should be a pension, whereas mid term should be put in a savings account with a high interest level (or investments – see below). Usually these have fixed terms; that is, you can't touch your money for X amount of years or else you lose interest. Short term should be in an easy-access account. Do your homework and shop around for savings accounts and pensions, because some really do have far better deals than others, and it pays to inform yourself.

Lazy girl's guide to savings and getting rich

Finally, before you start saving, work out if you are a risk-taker, because certain forms of investing, such as the stock market, are riskier than others, and, just to make the pot more tempting, these risky savings always come with a high earning potential. If you've always juggled your debts and thought something will just turn up to save you from bankruptcy, it's likely you have a risk-taking nature and may be eager to try these. The only problem is that whereas you do stand to make a large sum of money you also stand to lose a lot – and therein lies the rub! So invest wisely, because your goal is financial success not financial losses. Here's what to cast your eye over:

Cash or fixed-term deposit?

These accounts are made for smaller rather than larger investments and work well, because you can usually draw out your money whenever you want or with notice (so you don't lose the interest you've made on saving your money). Even if you're talking less than a £100 it's worth placing your money here, as even the smallest amount of cash will make more than it will sitting in a current/cheque account. To get the most out of these accounts, save every month or week and don't touch the money for as long as possible.

Scour the Internet for the best deals but only invest in reputable and known companies.

Shares

With shares you can make or lose a fortune, and that's the problem with them. If you're keen to make money quickly and know what you're doing you can make a tidy sum, especially as you now don't have to go through a broker to invest (you can do it through the Internet). Like any form of gambling, and that's what the stock market is, only invest as much as you can afford to lose, because there are no guarantees. And read up first to make sure you know what you are doing.

Managed funds

These are funds that have been invested into shares and property but are managed, and so it means you don't have to choose what to buy; you buy into investments a company has already set up. The downside is that you pay a fee for this (usually 5 per cent of your investment) and pay a fee to leave (again 5 per cent). Meaning, you have to make more than 10 per cent on whatever you've invested before it's even worth taking your money out.

Property

Most countries have had a bit of a property boom of late, and you may have friends who made a 'killing' and now own two properties or have sold a property at a healthy profit. It might seem like an excellent game to get into, but remember: although property prices are still high, the market is no longer booming in the massive way that it has been, although there is still plenty of money to be made. Also, only buy what you can afford, and make sure the property is in good repair, unless you have money put aside to do it up. Finally, think location, location, location … it's not what you buy but where you buy it that makes you money. So do your homework and research all your options and how much it will cost you in a deposit, taxes and legal fees before you move.

Pensions

Does the very word 'pension' send you to sleep? If so you're not alone, because most governments have a pretty hard time trying to persuade people to save for their old age. This is because most people don't want to look 40 years into the future, and most just assume that they'll be OK when that point comes around. Sadly, this isn't the case, and if you want your financial success to last throughout your life you have to have a pension, because it's a necessity, not a luxury, for your old age. So, if you only ever do one form of saving make sure it's this one!

So how about the getting rich part?

Well, sadly, this is not the bit where you find out how to lure a rich boyfriend, or break the bank at Vegas, but there are some tried and tested ways to make it financially and even get rich. Here are some ways other lazy girls have done it:

- Start your own business.

- Invest big time in property.

- Invent a new product.

- Write a best-seller.

- Win a major competition.

- Buy property aboard.

- Invest in the stock market.

- Become notorious for something.

- Get on TV.

- Work hard, invest, take measured risks and keep pushing your way up that career ladder!

20 ways

to be financially successful

1 Get a second job

Sounds like a lazy girl nightmare, but the fastest way to get rich is to increase your income by utilising your spare time. Think inside and outside of the box, and look for work that makes use of your current work skills, then hire yourself out or get a bar job, or even late-night reception work. Think you have no time? Well, think of all the time you spend watching TV, sitting in a bar and generally lolling about. If you're honest you probably have at least four hours a night to spare, not to mention weekends.

2 Invest wisely

Buying lottery tickets, investing in get-rich-fast schemes or even pyramid-selling schemes are not wise investments. In fact these schemes all aim themselves at the desperate, because they know people won't look at the details. To safeguard your investment, avoid anything that offers you miracle or speedy returns, and instead tread a more stable path via known institutions – like banks and building societies.

3 Start saving now

Studies show that most of us can save money if we simply cut back on non-necessities. If you're a paper or magazine junkie think about reading them online for free, swapping with friends, or simply going to a library to read them (again, free in most libraries). If you're a latte girl, either opt for one in the office, or have one at home. The same goes for bottled water – either go tap or buy a water filter. You'll be amazed at how much you save.

4 Shop smartly

Don't be a sucker for brands, as all they are doing is selling you a lifestyle through packaging. Instead, shop wisely and use own brands, or shop on the Internet for cheaper bargains. Buy during the sales, and work on the basis that if you have three pairs of jeans you don't need a new pair.

5 Take measured risks with your cash

As tempting as it may be to dabble in the stock market, or give your money to someone who says they can triple it in two weeks, remember it's impossible to get rich quick, so unless you can afford to lose money (and if you're currently reading this you can't) only take sensible risks with your cash.

6 Make spending hard

The harder you make it to spend, the more cash you'll have left in your pocket at the end of the month, so overhaul your social life and what you do with your cash. Stop going shopping because you're bored, and sitting in cafés all weekend. Also, help yourself by cutting up your credit and store cards or not taking them out with you so that you can avoid spontaneous got-to-have buys.

7 Lose the 'I deserve' mentality

This is the idea that somehow you deserve to wear designer clothes, eat at top-range restaurants and stay in five-star hotels even though you can't afford to. The problem with 'I deserve' is it gives you permission to spend more than you make and use up all your spare cash and borrowed cash, leaving you even further from your dream to be rich.

8 Think about what you're buying (all the time)

(That is, rate everything you want to buy out of ten before you part with cash.) Ask yourself 'How much do I really want/need this?' If you score less than seven don't buy it. If you score seven to eight, go away for a few hours and think about it; above eight you can buy it!

9 Delay gratification

The richer you want to be the more you have to delay gratification. Of course, living in poverty now to have zillions in the future is not the best way to live your life, but you do have to cut back, save and do without luxuries in order to have money to invest and, therefore, have money further down the line.

10 Make the most of your spare time

We all have unused skills that others could benefit from, whether they are a talent for painting and decorating, a talent for making things or even writing skills. You would be amazed at how many people make money from the things you take for granted. Research the Net to see how others make money, and consider offering yourself out for hire.

11 Don't be tempted by the more, more, more offers

Instead, always think twice before taking on more credit. The truth is that banks, retailers and credit card companies will endlessly offer you more money, because they make money from your debt. So it's not in their interests to have you solvent and financially successful. Whether you're tempted to increase your overdraft limit, or are offered more credit card money to borrow – just say NO!

12 Don't be flattered into spending

... or into getting a credit card with a massive limit. They aren't giving it to you because they like you but because they want you to get into more debt and spend the rest of your life paying them back so that they make money.

13 Be prepared to take small risks

Whether it's putting 120 per cent into your job (even though there's no guarantee you're going to get promoted), or taking on a job with more money (even though you're not sure it's completely you), or even investing your spare cash. You need to speculate to accumulate.

14 Know your worth

Don't be scared to ask for a pay rise, more of a bonus or even for overtime. If you work hard, or know you do more than they ask, then it's not cheeky to ask for higher dividends. Remember: they can only say no, and if they do, all you have to do is see it as a sign that it's time to move on.

15 Check your bills and statements

In fact, check everything you're asked to pay, from credit card receipts to restaurant bills, and look for additional charges that you haven't agreed to, over-charging and general mistakes. Who knows how much money you could be losing by not keeping an eagle eye on your accounts.

16 Keep a spending diary

(Also known as: keeping daily accounts of what goes out and what goes into your accounts.) Without a daily ledger how are you ever going to know how much you've got to spend, when your bills are coming out and what money you have to play with? Guesswork won't do it, and may well lead you right back into debt.

17 Avoid Sexually Transmitted Debt

(Also known as: having to pick up someone else's tab.) Relationships can be the number-one way to ruin yourself financially, especially if you're hooked up with someone who's incredibly good at spending your money, getting loans out in your name and encouraging you to buy things together. Don't let love blind you; always pay attention to what others are doing and suggesting what you should do with your cash.

18 Don't give up the day job

(As in, don't be so quick to put your job on hold for a career break, move to a less stressful one for less money and/or jack it in and travel round the world thinking you can always slip back into the job market.) While these are all options that can work, the reality is that what you earn today may not be what you earn tomorrow, so if you have a great job with a good earning potential, think long and hard before changing careers or taking a career break, and ask yourself whether you will financially regret it in five years' time? If the answer is 'maybe', really think about what you're doing.

19 Don't put all your eggs in one basket

(That is, don't put all your financial eggs in one basket and imagine that will do it.) Property, for example, is a great investment, but what would you do if the market crashed? Likewise, having a wealthy husband is great, but what if he lost his job or left you? Have you made provisions for your own financial security? If not, it's time to do so.

20 Protect your money

(As in, pay attention to what's happening to the financial market.) Do you need to move your money around to make it work better for you? Or take your money out of something that's losing money, or change jobs because your company is restructuring and you may be demoted? Always look ahead for potential financial hazards that might knock you sideways, so that you can sidestep them before they happen.

chapter five

Body
success

Some people may be wondering why a chapter on body and health would be in a book about success. Well, with a new study showing that 98 per cent of us hate our bodies, four out of ten of us are permanently on a diet, and most of us obsess about our bodies every 15 minutes, how you feel about your body has a pretty big impact on how you feel about the rest of your life. Let's face it, if you feel less than successful about your body, then you're going to feel less confident and less secure in public, less happy in a social situation where you're on show, and generally more tired and down on yourself than someone who feels they've beaten their body demons.

So, hands up if you're happy with your body! If you're a true lazy girl you probably aren't, but at the same time you can't face the idea of doing something that involves the words healthy food, diet, exercise and looking after your well-being, which is where this chapter comes in.

Body success is about many things, and how you choose to define your bodily successes is up to you. Your goals can be about losing weight, getting fit or simply silencing the inner food debate between the good you and bad you. Or it can be about stamping out horrible habits and getting your health under control; but whatever you decide it's going to be, you also have to accept that to feel successful about your body you need to improve your self-esteem and self-worth. In other words, you have to deal with the inner stuff, because if you don't do something about how you feel about the you on the inside then you're never going to feel successful about the you on the outside, whether you hit your kilo target, fit into a size 10 pair of jeans or get a place on the Olympic athletics team.

So, if you feel dumpy, lumpy and somewhat bloated right this second, here's your chance to make a successful attempt at getting your body in shape once and for all. Do it right and you're guaranteed to feel:

- Happier when naked.

- More comfortable with who you are in public.

- Less self-conscious in a social situation.

- More relaxed about your food choices.

- Less out of breath when you run upstairs.

- Less critical when you view your reflection in shop windows.

- More relaxed in photos.

- Less unhappy in your clothes.

- More confident in everyday life.

- Healthier and happier all round.

A good place to start in your attempt at body success is to do something about the neglected areas of your health regime, such as why you have no energy even to contemplate doing something about your body. Ask around those who are also body-negative and it's likely you'll find that despite body unhappiness they don't change their ways because (a) they can't be bothered; and (b) they don't see the point.

In reality they *can* see the point but just can't muster the energy to start thinking about it. Luckily, help is at hand. If you follow these very easy lazy girl measures you'll not only find you have some energy but also some much needed enthusiasm to think about, plan and go for some of your more serious body goals.

Lazy girl tip 1: have enough beauty sleep

You'd think as a lazy girl you'd be excelling in this area, but it's likely you're not. Most people skip sleep all week and then play catch-up at weekends, which not only knocks out your body clock but also makes you feel lethargic and even sleepier when you do wake up. For effective sleep, aim for seven solid hours a night (you'll know if it's too much because you'll either wake up early or find yourself unable to sleep when you do go to bed). To aid your sleep have a warm bath to make you feel drowsy (not a hot bath, as this has the opposite effect). Lower the room temperature –

a cool environment (around 16°C/61°F) improves sleep. Avoid caffeine (coffee, tea, diet drinks and some pain-killers) five hours before bed and don't go to bed hungry, but also don't eat a heavy meal two hours before bed, as this will compress the diaphragm and cause a restless night.

Lazy girl tip 2: silence the critic within

We all have this voice – it can be that of an ex, your mother or even someone you knew years ago. It's the nagging, nasty whine that tells you you're not good enough, that you eat the wrong foods, that you're lazy in a bad way and that you deserve body failure. Ironically, this is also the voice that pipes up when you try to do something about it. The gremlin that sniggers that you're going to fail when you try something new, or hints that you're going to embarrass yourself if you tell people you want to change, or encourages you to blow that diet.

The voice is your inner fear, the part of you that's afraid that maybe you can't change. Well, the good news is you can, because people change every single day no matter what their background or present circumstances. All you have to do is stop the voice by arguing back. Every time it says no, say yes and do it. Every time it puts you down, argue back and stand up for yourself. It's the road to better self-esteem, and you can find it.

Lazy girl tip 3: be real with yourself

'Who cares what I look like – it's what's inside that counts' is a popular refrain, and if that sounds like you, it's time to be real with yourself because you can't separate how you look on the outside from how you feel on the inside, as they are connected. In reality, what you're really saying is: I hate my body and have given up on it. So remember: body success is about all-over success, and to get there you have first to admit that you want to change. Say it loud and make it clear to yourself, because it's far more liberating (and less humiliating) than you think to admit finally to something you know you need and want to do, and start going for it.

tip

Forget willpower, and focus on what you want above everything to pull you through your body plan.

Lazy girl tip 4: stand tall

Do you have an ache in your shoulders, a tight, pulling feeling in your neck, a lower back that hurts if you stand too long or wear high heels? If so, you're not alone. Statistics show that on average 9.4 million of us spend over 75 per cent of our waking day sitting down, and the main culprits are the 18- to 29-year-olds. Thirty-eight per cent of respondents in this age range spend ten hours or more seated, compared to just 25 per cent of the over-fifties! This kind of sedentary lifestyle means your back and stomach muscles become severely underused. Roughly translated this means that your body is heading for disaster and you need literally to stand up, get active (30 minutes a day for an adult) and learn to maintain good posture.

Lazy girl tip 5: put your realistic goggles on

(Also known as: stop comparing yourself to others.) This is the kiss of death to body success, because if you're always looking at pictures of famous people and/or viewing yourself negatively in comparison to others, you're never going to feel good about yourself. So get naked and look at yourself in a mirror. Override the self-conscious side of you and focus on your body. Forget the ugly way X sticks out, or how small Y is, or even how Z could do with liposuction; instead, focus on what you like. What isn't so bad? What could you live with? What just needs a little work? What makes you feel sexy? What have you had compliments about? See, you're not so bad after all, are you?

Fitting the norm!

It's official: women are getting bigger, with the average being:

- Weight – 64kg (10 stone 2lb)
- Height – 1.62m (5ft 4in)
- Bra size – 34C
- Waist size – 86cm (34in)
- Hips – 102cm (40½in)

What is your idea of body success?

❛ My idea of body success used to be to get down to a size 8 and weigh under 9 stone [126lb/57kg] – it took me a while to realise that at 5ft 10in [1.77m] that wasn't going to be healthy. I'm now a size 12 and weigh 10 stone [140lb/63.5kg] and am really happy with that. Though sometimes I still look at super-thin girls and celebrities and think: I wish that could be me. ❜

Rebecca, 25

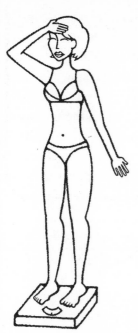

(Also known as: the great battle between The Real You v. The Fantasy You.) No matter how lazy a girl you currently are it's likely that somewhere in your mind lies the idea of the perfect you. This is the vision of how you'd look if you could be bothered to diet, exercise and work on your body goals instead of lying on the sofa. How The Fantasy You looks only you can say, but it's likely she's thin, she's long, she has pert breasts and no cellulite. Yes, she's Barbie Woman, and though most of us would argue to our deaths that we don't want to look like her, most of us have some variation of this image imprinted on our brains and use it to beat ourselves over the head with – usually on days when our hair goes crazy, our faces go spotty and we're faced with the muffin-belly overhang!

The problem is that as long as The Fantasy You is hanging about in the background you're never going to feel great about The Real You. In fact you're only ever going to feel 'OK' about yourself, or, as one lazy girl says, you'll only ever feel 'passable' – and, let's be honest, that's not body success, which means right now you have a choice:

1. You can either dump the fantasy and come up with a new vision for yourself and work towards that.

2. Or dump the fantasy and celebrate who you are right now.

Choice one above, although harder, is probably the easier road to take in the long run than choice two, because

tip

Get real about your shape. Your aim is to become the best you can be, not the best of someone else.

ditching the vision and loving who you are is tough when you really don't like your body. Meaning, no amount of platitudes or positive thinking will ever convince you that you're OK when you don't want to look the way you do, which is a long way of getting round to talking about the one thing that will change your body for ever – and that's effort! Hardly the lazy girl's mantra, but it is the key to getting the body you want. And the good thing about effort is, how much you put in is up to you. The equation is simple: huge effort equals huge results; small effort equals small results, both of which mean any effort of any sort equals a result.

It's up to you to decide what your finishing line is for body success, and then apply the effort needed to get there. For example, if you want to have the killer body of a very well-known female icon then you need to watch what you eat and work out 16 hours a day and, like her, you will look utterly fantastic. However, if you simply want to lose 6 or 7kg (1 stone/14lb) then all you need to do is cut back a little on what you like and get more active for 30 minutes every day (which is hardly going to kill you) and you'll reach your goal within eight weeks or less.

So, start by brainstorming your idea of body success. Ask yourself:

1. What would it take for me to feel happier about my body?

2. How could I achieve this?

3. What areas could I do with toning up?

4. How could I achieve this?

5. What areas could do with a makeover?

6. Who could help me do this?

7. What areas of my health do I need to boost, and why?

8. What's my deadline (goals don't work if you don't have a finishing point)?

If these questions don't help direct you where to go with your body success plan then it's likely you need to think about what you're trying to achieve and why. Like the person who fantasises about winning the lottery in order to be rich, and/or the person who sees being famous as a way to being successful at work, it's likely your vision of body success is not realistic. It's no good having some vague idea of what you'd like to look like based on a mixture of other people's bodies, plastic surgery and the hope that you'll just wake up one day and see someone else looking back at you. If you're 1.62m (5ft 4in) and pear-shaped you're never going to be a 1.8m (6ft) supermodel. Likewise, if you're tall and thin you're never going to be small and cute, but that doesn't mean you can't be sexy, strong, sensational-looking and happy with your body, no matter where your starting point is.

The key to body success is to take what you've got and to make the most of it. If that means honing and toning with exercise and dieting, so be it. If that also means primping and glossing, go for it too. Remember: it's not vain to want to make the most of yourself, and it's not negative to admit you'll never be model material. The trick is to be staggeringly honest with yourself and then apply effort to achieve the body success you want, whether it's slimmer legs, firmer breasts, glossy hair or a pert bottom.

You know your idea of body success is off-centre when:

- It involves plastic surgery.
- It involves zero effort.
- You're thinking: miracle or crash diet?
- You assume that one day it will just happen to you.
- You're hoping to get on a reality makeover show.
- You think bigger breasts will solve it all.
- You're always planning to start tomorrow.
- Your role model looks nothing like you.

Getting the body you want

Hopefully by now you have a more realistic idea of what you want to do with your body and why, so this is the part that helps you get from where you are now to where you want to be. Firstly, you've got to find your willpower. If weight loss is your goal, willpower is easy! You want to look better in clothes, so when you eat you use your vision of a slimmer you to enable you to eat healthily and so lose weight, and therefore look great in your clothes. Unfortunately, as we all know, willpower is just not that easy, because when it comes to eating we don't eat just because we're hungry, we eat for emotional reasons. These are usually when we're bored, need comfort, feel fed up and, the favourite, because we're treating ourselves, which means it's hard to maintain willpower when emotions step in and give you conflicting goals.

The answer to this dilemma is to forget willpower and think about what might motivate you above all other things to keep going. It can be a negative motivation: 'If I don't eat healthily I will always be single and weigh 120kg [18 stone 12lb/264lb] by this time next year'; or a positive one: 'If I do this I'll look great and feel confident enough to go for that promotion/ask X out/or start my own business.' By attaching a positive or painful image to what you want, and placing it at the pinnacle or bottom of your success tree you'll be more inclined to go after it and stay motivated when other lesser desires trickle in.

One thing you do have to learn when it comes to success, however, is the ability to delay gratification – if you can't see the bigger picture over the smaller one, you'll never be able to forgo the smaller one for what you really want. This applies whether you're going for business success, money success or love success, never mind body success. Meaning, you have to learn to avoid the comfort of your nightly chocolate bar in order to get the glory of a fabulous body! So help yourself by creating goals that smash instant gratification out of the water. For example, you want body success in three months because you:

tip

Results can be seen with exercise in as little as six weeks if you exercise regularly (three times a week for at least an hour each time).

- Intend to make an ex jealous (and sorry he left you) at your birthday party.

- You want to wow everyone at a wedding.

- You want to look sexy on the beach.

- You want to walk into a new job looking fabulous.

- You want to pull at the Christmas party.

- You want to prove to everyone that you're more than they think you are.

How to be successful on a diet

It's easier than you think and doesn't involve starvation and locking yourself away for months.

Step 1: be honest about how much you eat

If you feel you don't eat much and yet have steadily gained weight over the last few years, then you need to become aware of what you're eating and how much you're eating, because these two things alone determine your weight gain. The first thing you need to realise is that not all foods are made the same and, generally, it's the food that tastes good that usually packs the most on the calorie front. Meaning, those are the foods that cram an almighty amount of energy into a small area, which is why even eating a small amount (and thereby thinking you're not eating much) can cause you to gain weight. To help yourself see where you might be adding silent calories without knowing, keep a food diary and note where your weak spots lie. Also note down every bite, every snack, every piece of food while you're cooking and every drink you slurp. This technique will not only help you to be honest about what you eat but will also help you to create a healthier food plan for body success.

Step 2: stop going on mad diets

We're all tempted by mad diets because the thought that we could lose weight easily and quickly while eating our favourite foods, or a certain food, is tantalising. However, if you can reel off five diets without even thinking, and your bookshelf is full of every get-thin-fast book known to humankind, then you're a lazy girl diet-junkie and need to go into diet rehab. Firstly, get rid of the idea that there is a miracle diet out there for you. The only effective way to body success on the weight-loss front is to lose weight steadily through healthy eating – that means less of the rubbish and more of the good stuff. Push your body through crash diets and you'll mess up your metabolism and make losing weight an even tougher job than it has to be.

Step 3: eat like a healthy person

Healthy people don't police what goes into their mouths, feel guilty when they eat something 'bad' and skip meals because they want to lose weight. They eat when they're hungry and stop when they're not. They also eat three proper meals a day including breakfast. Which is why if you want body success it pays to focus on your morning meal, especially if you want to lose weight and get through the morning in a good mood. The reason behind this thinking is simple: your body needs fuel/energy in the morning because it hasn't eaten for at least 10 hours. Deprive it of energy and it will run on empty and then retaliate at 11.00 a.m., and lunchtime, and pretty much all day.

Step 4: have realistic goals

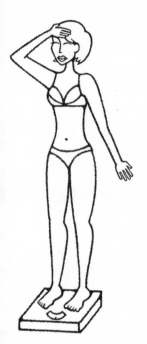

Aiming to lose 25 kilos (3 stone 13lb/55lb) in two months is not a realistic goal, and is one that will scupper even the best laid plans, because there is no way you can reach it in such a short space of time. Meaning, you'll feel cheated, get fed up with what you're doing and veer off-course and probably into a cake shop. Diet goals, like goals for any area of success, need to be viable, achievable and realistic. This means: think of your lifestyle, your end goal and your personality, and work out what course of action works best for you. Cold turkey works best for some people – whereby you cut out all your temptations for a month and then introduce them back in moderation – whereas others find group weight loss more motivating, or a structured diet at home more effective. Choose the plan that suits your character best and your chances of reaching your goal will multiply.

Step 5: take small steps

Rome wasn't built in a day, and neither will your new body be, but body success can be achieved with a simple strategic plan that you can put into action on a daily basis. Think healthy eating, exercise, motivation, effort, and short- and long-term goals. Although, be aware that in any plan there comes a point where you think 'Stuff it! I'm giving up.' Weirdly this usually happens just as you're about to make a breakthrough of some sort, which means no matter how low you are, don't give up. Find something else to do, have a bath, slap a face pack on, go for a walk (without cash so you can't buy anything to eat) and just do something that takes your mind off eating. If you're truly having a bad day, give in to it in a small way and move on. What matters is always what you do next – not what you've done already!

How to be successful with exercise

The good news for any lazy girl currently flagging under the idea of joining a gym or making her legs run is that you don't have to be an ex-PE whizz-kid with silver cups and team medals under your arm to be good at exercise. Why? Well, because the idea is to get fit, not be picked first for teams, or run a marathon, which means your main worry should not be about coming last but simply about getting your butt out there in the first place.

Sadly, for many people, the idea of exercise is more abhorrent than a diet, which is why people start diets every day and people only tend to start exercising either at New

Year or when the beach season cometh. This is down to one simple reason: in order to exercise you need to take action, which means you actually need to move, whereas to diet you can just stare morosely into the fridge all day at a tub of cottage cheese and do nothing. Both equal weight loss; HOWEVER, studies show that people who exercise win on the body success front in the long run, because exercisers:

- Have leaner bodies than people who diet because muscle takes up a third of the space of fat.

- Have more self-esteem and confidence because their bodies feel stronger.

- Keep weight off for longer than dieters.

- Feel more positive than dieters.

- Feel great in general, as exercise releases feel-good endorphins.

- Have better sex lives (more energy, more enthusiasm).

- Are healthier – on average the risk of having a heart attack is reduced by about a third in people who exercise.

So how do you go from a couch potato to a successful exerciser in the least painless way possible?

Step 1: find your motivation

This is about body success, so what is it about exercise that will help you to fulfil your idea about body success?

Well, if you want a more sculpted body, or a more defined stomach, exercise is your answer. If you want more stamina, and a healthy, young look, exercise is your answer. If you want to run for the bus without passing out, try on clothes that fit and feel and look sexy – exercise is your answer!

And the real key to successful exercising is to find a sport or activity that suits you and inspires you, as well as getting you results. So, think outside of your current box – do you want to learn to run, dance, try martial arts, snowboard, swim or even become as bendy as a yoga woman? If so, you can, and, contrary to popular belief, it won't take years and years to get there. Results can be seen with exercise in as little as six weeks, if you exercise regularly (three times a week) and work out to 70 per cent of your maximum heart rate; that is, to a point where you can talk, but it's an effort.

To motivate yourself, create a realistic vision of how you'd like your new body to look (guide yourself with a realistic vision of your shape and other people's success stories). Read fitness books or find a trainer to motivate you, or ask the help of someone in the know so that you can put together a workout plan that (a) you want to do; (b) is different every day; and (c) can easily become part of your life, so that you have no excuse than to go after your goal.

‘ *I was always a serial dieter. I would drop weight, and then slowly put it on again, and I could never keep it off. Then a friend suggested I exercise to help stabilise, so I started running. Now I haven't gained weight for over two years.* ’

Helen, 28

Step 2: make it a habit

This is vital: if you don't make exercise a habit you will never maintain your body success plan. Think you can't make it a habit? Well, eating chocolate at 4.00 p.m. every day is a habit, having a takeaway every Friday night is a habit – which proves that habits are easily created without your even thinking. Studies from the US show that all it takes is three to four weeks to create a habit that you'll stick to. That's 30 days out of your whole life (think how long you've been talking about doing this). The 30-day rule is simple: pick three days a week, and every week at the same time on these days do your exercise of choice. For a whole month, be clear with friends and family that you will not be tempted away, no matter whether you're tired, eager to sleep or have a very important social engagement. When tempted to break your pact, remind yourself that you're only sabotaging yourself – after all, every time you break it means you have to start again!

Step 3: when the going gets tough, keep going

Of course there will be times when you have a setback, such as when you're injured, unwell or work gets in the way, but it is essential to jump back on the wagon and keep going. Life doesn't run smoothly for anyone and it doesn't take much to give us an excuse to back down. To help yourself, rope in some support from friends who work out, seek out a new class or a trainer, and pay for things in advance (an amazing way to motivate yourself to go). Above all, keep reminding yourself of your plan, your vision and how you'll feel by the end of the year (or whatever your deadline is), when you reach your goal and achieve the ultimate in body success.

Step 4: rate your successes

In order to keep going and to motivate yourself to go, it's essential that you see successes along the way, so set yourself a series of short-term and long-term goals. Short-term goals should be losses in weight or centimetres (inches), a drop in dress size, an alleviation of a specific ache or pain, or strengthening in a certain area of fitness (such as your back gets better, your body doesn't ache so much after exercising, and you can actually breathe when you stop running). Long-term goals are: you have your main goal at the end, and along the way you can have larger markers, such as a specific weight, or a specific exercise challenge (such as 'I will run 5km [3miles]' or 'I will go on a yoga retreat'). Even larger goals, which may seem impossible now but will seem more achievable as you get fitter, are entering a half-marathon, deciding to go for a specific accreditation in a sport, or training to be a fitness or yoga teacher (all achieved by ex-lazy girls).

Step 5: challenge yourself

Finally, be aware that, with exercise, when you get into the swing of it you need to keep challenging yourself to feel inspired – whether you're a secret star or someone who loves it but fumbles through. Whenever an exercise gets easy and you don't feel it afterwards, ensure that you bump it up a notch or two so that you still feel challenged by what you're doing. In terms of body success this will increase your fitness and keep your body looking fantastic, but more importantly, it will ensure you continue to feel successful, because the weird thing about success is, whenever you reach one summit you'll find you get your much-deserved high, but to carry on getting it you have to (and will want to) keep pushing the summit higher.

Step 6: make activity part of your life

In order to achieve body success for life you have to see exercise and activity as a part of your life for life, not something you're doing to get a life. If those words stick in your throat, remind yourself that exercise is something that can be enjoyed, not just sweated through. Make it more fun by starting your own running group with friends, hiring a yoga teacher to teach a group of you, or borrowing a fitness video and working through it twice a week with your best mate. That aside, make sure you get active every day, alongside your three weekly workouts – whether it's climbing stairs, walking to work, carrying shopping or walking across the office instead of sending an email; because all it takes is one hour of activity a day (that's 20 minutes before work, 20 minutes at lunchtime and 20 minutes post-work) to keep you healthy and body fit. Get used to moving and it will be less of a climb to get used to exercising, and less of an effort to find body success.

How to be successful with self-esteem

Unlike dieting and exercise, self-esteem is a harder concept to grasp in terms of body success, especially if you've been adept at giving yourself a hard time for years, and are comfortable (albeit in a painful way) with this mode of thought. If so, it's time for a wake-up call of the emotional kind, because otherwise:

- No matter how great you look, you're never going to feel as if you've achieved body success.

- No matter what dress size you buy, you aren't going to feel great.

- No matter how much you weigh, you're not going to feel good or happy.

So what is self-esteem? Well, it's the part of you that gives yourself value, knows you're worth more than what someone else tells you, and helps you to stand up for yourself. Whereas we're born with heaps of it, over the years our esteem gets eroded by parents, teachers, comments from friends and even lovers, and slowly we can find that our vision of ourself goes from being strong and confident to fragile and based on other people's views. If you're someone who always remembers the insults and throws away the compliments, puts herself down all the time, and thinks she deserves less than others, you have a bad case of low self-esteem.

To boost your self-esteem you need to:

Re-educate yourself

The best way to do this is to hang around women who have good self-esteem. These women are easy to spot: they're generous, fun and feel good about themselves and their lives. They don't put themselves down, but at the same time they don't go around telling everyone they are gorgeous and fabulous. Watch how they talk about themselves and react around others, and sneak tips off them.

Learn to appreciate things about yourself other than your looks

As we've said earlier, body success is not just about having a killer beach body and sexy looks, it's about feeling good about yourself for who you are as well as for what you look like. Meaning, you need to focus on other areas besides diet and exercise. What can your body do besides sit on the couch? What talents do you secretly (or not so secretly) possess, what strengths do you have, what physical achievements can you get from your body? Get out there and try, so that you can start seeing other things in your body besides beauty.

Stop with the lazy thinking

Lazy thinking is imagining you'll feel good about yourself once you lose weight, have firm arms and hit a size X in the shops. Lazy thinking is also imagining no one knows what it's like for you and worrying that people are judging you because you don't look perfect. If that's a taste of your daily thought process, just STOP! Take the focus off you and look externally. Firstly, no one's perfect – look around you on the bus and see that the world is made up of all kinds. Secondly, the only person who's judging you for not being perfect is you, which means you can stop at any time. Change the record before it bores you to death and think body success, not body bitching!

Appreciate your body and your mind

That is, appreciate your body for what it can do now, how healthy it is, and how far it's brought you in life. It may not be where you want it to be yet, but it's not all bad, and neither are you. We all veer off-course in life and wake up feeling unfit and unhealthy, as well as stupid about the choices we've made, but rather than use that to make yourself feel bad, change the record and remember the only way is up!

20 ways
to feel body success

1 Stop comparing your body to everyone else's
It's the number-one way to help you to feel happier, look fabulous and generally be the most gorgeous person in the room. If you find yourself doing it consciously, make yourself focus on something boring – like your fingernail – breathe deeply three times and then look up and think of two positive things about yourself.

2 Monitor your progress
Not to see how far you've got to go, but to see how far you've come. This is essential if you want to succeed, because it fuels the motivation you need to keep going when things get tough. Research shows that people who track their successes and failures tend to reach their goals *and* get there faster than others.

3 Take a month off to make it work
What's 30 days (four weeks) in a lifetime of moaning about your body? It sounds severe but the best way to

achieve body success is to take yourself out of your normal social life for a month and stick rigidly to your body success plan so that (a) no one can tempt you away; (b) you create new habits; and (c) you see amazing results in just 30 days. Remember: in just one month you can lose 5.5kg (12lb 2oz), gain lean muscles, lose inches, change food habits and improve your skin and hair.

4 Believe you can do it

This is a major factor in any pursuit of success you undertake. To start believing in yourself, first remind yourself of all your past successes in this field (previous weight loss, fitness, being on a school team, and so on) and then talk to people who have achieved what you're going for so that you can see you're not so different.

5 Don't work on a reward basis

This is especially important when it comes to body success, as it's likely your rewards will be of the lazy and food variety, which will go against your aims. The other problem with rewarding yourself for every goal you reach is that you'll find that you lose sight of your overall goal (body success) and instead start making your rewards larger and larger, and so lose motivation altogether.

6 Avoid distraction

Your mind is a clever thing and can easily distract you from the things you know you should be doing, which is why when it comes to success it pays to focus on one thing at a time. If body success is your goal, forget writing your best-seller, or becoming a millionaire by the time you're 30 years old, and focus, focus, focus on the goal in hand.

7 Focus on the solution not the problem

OK, you need to lose 20kg (3 stone/44lb), and it's your fault because you eat too much, don't exercise and drink alcohol all the time, if only you'd ... Stop right there! If you want to change things you have to think about the solution, not the problem.

8 Ditch the takeaways

The fastest away to avoid weight gain is to ditch all your takeaway menus and take the Indian takeaway number off speed dial. This way you can't be tempted to order in when you're tired, fed up or looking to cheat on your food plan. And even if you do find yourself walking towards the takeaway, at least you will be getting some exercise.

9 Get some good underwear

Think of it like scaffolding – in order to keep your body looking good and feeling firm, it pays to have great underwear that fits well, doesn't pinch or cut into your skin and smoothes your body down under your clothes. It's a cheat's guide but it's also invaluable whether you've reached body success or not.

10 Rate your hunger before you eat

This is the ideal way to check why you're eating and ensure you eat only when you're hungry. The next time you pick up a packet of crisps or a biscuit, stop and ask yourself how hungry you are. If it's below a seven out of ten, don't eat it and wait until you score closer to ten.

11 Challenge yourself to do something physical

In most cases when someone is hard on their body, they rarely challenge themselves to do something amazing to prove they're wrong. So forget being bad at PE and having the stamina of a gnat, and challenge yourself to learn a new sport (dancing included) or run a race so that you can really push your body to the limit and see what it can do.

12 Try on a new look

Like trying on a new sport, changing your look can also help you to achieve and feel body success. Grab a handful of clothes in colours you rarely wear and head into a shop changing room to give yourself a styling session. If you're stuck for where to start, grab an assistant, or your best friend, for help – and experiment!

13 Don't let other people's opinions matter more than your own

Lots of people have their own agendas, so when you're attempting to change and aim for body success, don't listen to the people around you. Go by what feels right in your gut. If you're doing this for you, then do it regardless of what they might be saying.

14 Give yourself a new label

Are you the prototype lazy girl, or Ms Fat-Bum girl or Mrs Blobby? Whatever you call yourself in private or public, it's time to give yourself a new label and use it. Choose one that inspires you, motivates you and brings you closer to your body-success goal, and every time you refer to yourself use your new label.

15 Aim to make a small improvement each day

Whether that's eating your five portions of fruit and vegetables, drinking 1.5 litres (2¾ pints) of water or giving yourself five compliments, aim to improve something about your body awareness every day from now on.

16 When in doubt ask for help

You don't have to do it alone, and with body success there are about a billion experts out there desperate to help you to win. So if you can't exercise efficiently think about getting a personal trainer, and if you can't afford that then try an exercise class, or borrow a book from the library written by an expert. The same goes for diet advice and self-esteem: find a mentor, read up on it and when in doubt ask for help.

17 Get real about your flaws

Specifically, be realistic about your perceived flaws; otherwise, you will spend the rest of your life hating yourself, and your body success will always feel but a distant dream. And remember: the more you focus on something, the bigger it gets, whether it's a problem, a facial scar or a spot!

18 Make the best of what you've got

We all have areas of our body that are good, whether it's legs that make up for no waist, breasts that give us curves or hair that's the envy of everyone. Accentuate the positive and learn to like your good bits so that you can then just get on and deal with the parts you want to hone into shape.

19 Don't take on someone else's neurosis

Whingeing is addictive, and being around people who constantly bemoan their weight or flabby bits can be contagious and make you feel as if you're in the same boat. So either stay away from them or limit their whinge time with you.

20 Change is within your grasp

No matter how much you hate your body right this second, you can make a decision to change and immediately start to be a different person on a different path. Remember: people suddenly become fit after a lifetime of lethargy, or thin after a lifetime of diets, or suddenly feel good about themselves for no other reason that they've chosen to. If they can do it, you can, too.

chapter six

The A–Z of how to be extremely successful in life

*L*uck, guts and winning the lottery aside, here are all the components a lazy girl needs to be successful:

Ambition

A goal, an objective, an aspiration and/or desire – call it what you may – but in order to be successful you have to have ambition, because it's this that will drive you forwards and upwards. Think you're not the ambitious type? Then you need to ask yourself (a) why you're reading this book (chances are you are actually ambitious, but you're what's known as passively ambitious); and (b) how you hope to be successful without having the essential go-getting drive? If you're stumbling over this one, simply learn to use your dreams as a motivational tool rather than as an escape from your daily life and you'll find your ambition. If you're ambition starved (and you'd be surprised at how many people are) start by thinking about what you want from your life. Write a dream list that states your ideal job, relationship, financial situation and social life, and then focus on the one ideal that makes you feel the most excited and happy. From this point, start building a plan that focuses on you achieving your dream, aka your main ambition.

Bounce back

(As in, have the ability to bounce back from any disaster, be it emotional, work, health or financial.) This one's hard because when tough things happen they rock our self-confidence and make us feel as if we should give up and not expect so much from life. However, the key to true and lasting success is to have what's known as lots of resilience! None of us can stop disaster from occurring (jobs can take a downward turn, lovers leave and savings funds go bust). When this happens it's how you choose to make your comeback that will determine your long-term success. Get stuck in the quagmire of defeat and all that will happen is you'll stay where you are: defeated and depressed. Instead, bounce back from even the smallest of defeats and you'll feel more able to cope with the larger ones. This means, stop whingeing and analyse what went wrong. Figure out what you can learn from it and choose to focus on the things you can change, not the stuff that's happened and is now in your past. Remember: you can't change what's happened, but you can influence what will happen now.

tip

Even the laziest girl can find her inner ambition – just think about what you want from life and then how you're going to get it!

Courage

Being courageous is not about having zero fear, it's about being able to move ahead even if you're afraid. And to be successful this is exactly what you have to do even if this means gritting your teeth, silencing your hammering heart and jumping in with your eyes closed. The truth is that success takes huge amounts of courage, because it's guts that get you to the glory. So to find your courage, build a fear pyramid with your scariest goal at the top and your smallest at the bottom. Then every day/week make yourself grit your teeth and face a fear. It's not only a good way to find your inner pluck but it also builds up your daring gene, making you less fearful of failure and more likely to go after what you want.

Direction

(As in make sure you have one, especially if you're aiming for success.) Saying 'I want to be successful in love, money and work' is too vague a goal, you need to have a specific direction to head for, such as I want to be married in a year, I want to be solvent or have savings in six months and/or I want to own my own company in five years' time. Have a direction and you'll literally know where you're heading at all times, so that you won't be distracted to head off-course, get lost along the way or find yourself confused halfway along your journey.

> *tip*
>
> Everyone's afraid when they have something to lose – the trick is to move forwards despite your anxieties.

Ego

Why ego you may be thinking? Well, whereas ego (as in 'She's got a colossal ego') can be defined as having an inflated feeling of pride and superiority, ego is also about believing in who you are, and seeking out what your inner voice tells you that you want. In terms of success this means working out what you want and why. Contrary to popular belief, if your ego says you want and need praise for your achievements or need acclaim in your life, go for it. It's not egotistic to seek approval if that's your definition of success.

Faking it

With success there is always a certain amount of faking, whether it's faking courage to chat someone up, faking that you've got ideas for a new job or even faking that you've got what it takes to run your own business. What's more, all successful people fake it to a certain extent because sometimes that's what it takes to get a foot in the door. However, there is a world of difference between faking it and lying. Faking is about skirting over a few details because you know you can do something or be something, whereas lying is purposefully leading someone astray. If you are going to exaggerate you need to be willing to catch up fast. Decide wisely because it will come back to haunt you.

Game plan

A game plan is your personal strategy that gets you from where you are now to where you want to be in a set period of time. For example, if you want to lose weight and get fit your game plan should obviously involve a diet, exercise and motivational strategy that gets you moving. If you want to fall in love, your strategy should involve widening your social circle and dating more people. To create your perfect game plan, first think about what you want, then what it will take to get you there, and finally what you can do on a weekly and daily basis to get you there. Write it down and stick it somewhere you can see it every day, so that you actually follow it.

Habits

Horrible habits, idle habits, and sofa-dozing habits – it's these lazy girl habits that will keep you from success. Which means that if you're aiming for victory you have to take a long, hard look at your current habits and work on overhauling them. The good news is you don't have to bin all your lazy traits to be successful, but you do have to temper them with more zealous habits that make you get up and go. The good news is that research from the US shows it takes only 30 days to cement a new habit into your psyche, so even if the start is tough, make sure you do something new every day, such as send out your CV, or scan an Internet dating site, and by the month's end your new habits will be set in stone.

Integrity

Whether you're aiming for love success, financial kudos or career victory always think about keeping your integrity intact; that is, be true to yourself and who you are, or else you'll regret it when you get to your goal. If anything, refusing to compromise your ethics/morals will be your greatest asset when it comes to being successful, because it ensures that when you do reach your goals you don't feel you have cheated yourself or others and so can enjoy your success guilt-free.

Jealousy

When you want success it's natural to feel jealous of those who have it, and even a little bit gutted when someone reaches one of your goals before you. However, jealousy is a fairly destructive emotion, and if you sit with it for too long it can immobilise you, so the trick is to use it to your advantage. If you feel jealous because a friend has lost weight, got engaged and won the job lottery, use it to motivate yourself to get moving, and remember: just because she has what you want, it doesn't mean that (a) you can't get it too; and (b) that she has somehow stolen it from you.

Knowledge

Information and knowledge are power, and that works for every area of your life whether you're thinking dating, more money or career success. Whatever your goal it pays to increase your knowledge base to get there. For example, if you want to write a novel, get reading and do a creative writing course; if you want to find Mr Right, work out where the best place to find dates is and how to flirt more effectively. And keep reminding yourself that you can never know too much, so don't assume you already have all the knowledge you'll ever need to get where you want to be.

tip

Successful people know to suck up every morsel of knowledge that comes their way because they never know when they might need to use it.

Love

When it comes to success, love is an important component, because in order to feel truly successful you have to love what you're going after. (If you don't, what's the point of going after it?) This doesn't mean you have to love every part of your game plan, after all if you're after a killer body it's likely you won't love your exercise regime or dieting goals, and if you're aiming to be rich, living to a budget isn't going to be something you adore. However, make sure your overall goal is something you love and adore because then it will make all the parts you loathe bearable and easier to get through.

Money

Contrary to popular belief you don't need to have money to be successful, although it does help, or rather it does help to know where you can get it from or borrow it from if you're aiming for a success in something like your own business. However, having said that, money isn't in itself a road to success, and having lots of it won't make you feel successful unless it's tied to some other kind of achievement! Financial security, however, is a key trait of success, as knowing you can pay your bills, generally buy what you need and drive a nice car without worrying does tend to indicate that you've made it.

Network

Unfortunately, networking has a bit of a nasty corporate ring to it and conjures up pictures of having to make endless small talk over drinks with people you have nothing in common with. But no matter how much you hate the idea of networking for success, connections count, and not just in the career arena. Take relationships, for example; if you're single the more people you know and the more people who know you are actively looking for love, the higher your chances of being introduced to someone. This in turn can give you an advantage, and open up opportunities for you that you may not have known existed.

> *tip*
>
> The best lazy way to network is simply to be nice to every new person you meet so that when people refer to you in conversation they have something nice to say about you.

Optimism

By now you should know that if you're looking for success it pays to be optimistic; as in have a positive and forward-thinking attitude. Expecting the worse, and being generally pessimistic about your chances of success just proves to be a self-fulfilling prophecy mainly because your attitude influences your behaviour. Think yourself into a failure rut and that's where you'll be. On the other hand, believe you can do more and get more, and that's what you'll get, because it's this that will drive you towards your success goals.

People-watch

Even the laziest of the lazy can do this one because all it entails is watching how successful and unsuccessful people do things in life. People-watching works because you can learn a lot from the way people behave and the decisions they choose to make in their daily life. Watch long enough and you'll see that successful people have common traits, such as effective time management, planning skills and organisat-ional aptitude, whereas unsuccessful people tend to procrastinate, work without a game plan and fly by the seat of their pants. Look and learn is the key here, and work out what you then need to do to change or improve your strategy.

Query everything

Never ever be afraid to ask questions and query things, even if you fear your questions will make you look stupid, because the only way to learn, and discover what works and what doesn't, is to garner as much information as possible from everyone you meet. Get into the habit of asking at least five questions a day (of yourself and others). Whether it's 'Am I doing the right thing?' or 'How did you do that?' or 'What have I learned today?'

Realism

Dream big but also keep your feet firmly on the ground at the same time. When it comes to success you have to have a realistic attitude towards your abilities and dreams, and know what your strengths and weaknesses are, otherwise you're asking for a lot of wasted time feeling depressed.

Being realistic, however, doesn't mean giving up on what you want, it just means assessing and tinkering with your game plan. For example, just because you've been on two dates and haven't yet found Mr Right or can't lose 20kg (3 stone/44lb) in six weeks doesn't mean your goals are unrealistic; it's more a case of your time frame that is unrealistic; change that and your unrealistic goal becomes realistic.

Skills

(As in get loads of skills and not just for work success.) You need skills in life to be successful at anything – whether that's finding love (flirting skills, communication skills, sex skills), getting fit (healthy-eating skills, exercise skills, motivational skills), being financially astute (budgeting skills, saving skills and stock market skills). And no matter how many skills you have, it's always worth brushing up on them, building on them and making sure you keep them up to date. As for working out where to get them from, skills can be gathered from anywhere, role models, books, colleagues and even the Internet, so you have no excuse when it comes to bumping up your quota.

Time management

It's vital to look at where your time goes, because this is an important element of living a successful life. If you find that time just slips through your fingers you need to work out where it's going, because it's likely that your bad time management is stopping you from reaching your goals and doing all the things you want to do. Start by being realistic about your time and prioritising what's essential and important on a day-to-day basis.

tip

The aim is to time manage daily so that the important tasks (in whatever arena you decide is important) are achieved with time to spare for the more lazy aspects of life.

Unusual approaches

To be successful it pays to take whatever unusual approach you can because whereas there are set objectives that can start you on the path to success, mixing them with your own unique approach also works wonders and helps you to stand out from the crowd. Take the woman who lost 30kg (4 stone 10lb/66lb) just eating fast food for breakfast, lunch and dinner (not recommended), the woman who said yes to every date for a year and found her Mr Right in the process and the successful career woman who jacked in her very successful city job to sell swanky make-up ranges (her first love) and became a millionaire in the process. The trick is to do what you have to do and to follow your gut instinct, like these women have, and see where it takes you.

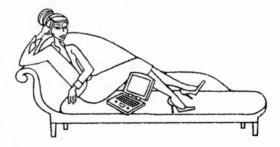

Visualise success

Positive visualisation is about having the right mental attitude to success. Meaning, seeing yourself as successful and your goals as successful rather than as someone who can't ever get what they want. The best way to train yourself to visualise positively is to start small. The next time you feel nervous about heading into a meeting or a date, focus on a positive outcome. See yourself performing well and your boss/date being great, and you'll be amazed at how this affects your behaviour during the actual meeting/date. Positive visualisation works because we behave outwardly in the manner we imagine, which is why when we focus on things crumbling they usually do, and when we see ourselves winning we win!

Willpower

To reach success a certain amount of delayed gratification and enforced willpower has to be displayed whether you're trying to avoid the foods you love to get fit, making yourself go out instead of staying in so you can meet someone, and/or sticking to a budget in order to get solvent.

Sadly, the problem with willpower is that when it comes to fighting temptation most of us have a real problem locating it and making it work for us, so the key is not to deny yourself what you want or what you want to do (which only makes you focus on it more and so erodes your willpower), but to motivate yourself not to want it in the first place by imagining yourself achieving your goal. This then makes it easier to stick to your plan and kick your willpower into action.

Zzzz – get some sleep

Success is hard work and even more tiring when you get there, so to make sure you're at your optimum strength, work on getting the right sleep balance; that is, don't over-sleep, or skip sleep. If you need to get up early, go to bed earlier (yes, sorry, it means cutting down on your social life), and if you need to work late, make sure it's not simply down to bad time management. As one successful entre-preneur recently said, 'If you're working until 2.00 o'clock every morning, you're doing something wrong.' So make sure you have what's known as a good work-life balance, as no area of your life should outbalance the other. This way you'll have the energy to enjoy your much worked-for success!

Resources

Career

UK
Personality test sites:
www.psi.com
www.thepsychometricscentre.co.uk
www.peoplemaps.co.uk
www.bbc.co.uk/science/humanbody/mind/index_surveys.
shtml

UK Online Careers Library: www.careers.lon.ac.uk

Australia
Information for job seekers: www.careersonline.com.au

New Zealand
Information and guidance: www.kiwicareers.govt.nz

South Africa
For help with jobs and careers: www.careers.org/reg/
cint-safrica-jobs-and-careers-in-south-africa

North America
Tests to help you find the career you want:
www.mindtools.com

Canada
The Canadian Association of Career Educators and
Employers (CACEE) provides information, advice, and
other services to employers, career services professionals,
and students: www.cacee.com

Love

UK
Relate offers advice, relationship counselling, sex therapy,
workshops, mediation, consultations and support face to
face, and through its website: www.relate.org.uk

Australia
Relationships Australia is an organisation that offers
resources to couples, individuals and families to help
enhance and support relationships:
www.relationships.com.au

New Zealand
Relate. For relationship services working with individuals,
couples, families, children, young people and the elderly:
www.relate.org.nz

North America
Council for Relationships, for couples' counselling:
www.councilforrelationships.org

For relationship counselling: www.psychologistsusa.com

Canada
For relationship counselling: www.psychotherapists.ca

Finance

UK
Consumer Credit Counselling Service (CCCS).
A free, confidential advice service for people in debt:
www.cccs.co.uk
Tel: 0800 138 1111

Credit Action. A national charity that aims to help people
educate themselves about money:
www.creditaction.org.uk
Tel: 01522 699777

FCL Debt Clinic. A free, confidential helpline offering
advice and solutions, including supervised arrangements
with creditors: www.fcl.org.uk
Tel: 0800 716239 (freephone helpline,
open 9.00 a.m. – 9.00 p.m., Monday–Friday)
Email: help@debtclinic.co.uk

Money Saving. Advice from Martin Lewis:
www.moneysavingexpert.com

National Debtline. Phone service offering advice and self-help information packs to those in debt:
www.nationaldebtline.co.uk
Tel: 0808 808 4000 (free and confidential)

Australia
A non-profit organisation representing Consumer Credit Counseling: www.debt-management-foundation.com

Legal aid: www.legalaid.nsw.gov.au
Tel: 1800 808 488

New Zealand
Citizen Advice Bureaux: www.cab.org.nz
Tel: 0800 367 222

North America
Family Credit Counseling: www.familycredithelp.org
Tel: 1 800 304 2369

Free advice on how to reduce debt:
www.800creditcarddebt.com

Canada

CanLaw. Help with information on credit, debt consolidation, credit counselling or bankruptcy: www.canlaw.com/credit
Tel: 1 888 527 8999

Body

UK

British Nutrition Foundation: www.nutrition.org.uk
Tel: 0207 404 6504

Gyms

Cannons: www.cannons-health-club.co.uk
David Lloyd Clubs: www.davidlloydclubs.co.uk
Holmes Place: www.holmes-place.co.uk
LA Fitness: www.lafitness.co.uk
Walking: www.walking.org

Australia

Fitness site: www.healthandfitness.com.au
Fitness tips: www.fitnessaustralia.com.au
Personal trainers and gyms: www.fitnessonline.com

New Zealand

Health and fitness tips: www.everybody.co.nz
Health, nutrition and fitness tips: www.gymfit.co.nz

South Africa

Nutrition: www.bodyline.co.za

Gyms, fitness tips, stockists, and yoga and Pilates: www.fitnesszone.co.za

North America

American Council on Exercise: www.acefitness.org

Healthy eating site: www.dieticians.ca

Health and fitness tips: www.shape.com

Gyms: www.healthclubdirectory.com/health_clubs/Canada

Index